LETTERING

LINKS

LETTERING

Edition 2010

Author & production: Daniel Blanco
Graphic design : Oriol Vallés
Text: Jay Noden, Jacobo Krauel, Lidia Barros, Raimondo Pibiri

© Carles Broto i Comerma (work conception)

Jonqueres, 10, 1-5

08003 Barcelona, Spain

Tel.: +34-93-301-21-99

Fax: +34-93-301-00-21

info@linksbooks.net

www.linksbooks.net

LETTERING

LINKS

Introduction

Without entering into hierarchies, we could say that graphic design has more in common with pottery than it has with painting; that designing a website is closer to repairing a shoe than conceiving an opera.

This seems to have been well understood by a generation of post-modern designers who have gone beyond computer technology. They have seen its obvious limitations. Computers are no longer the be all and end all; they have become simply another tool in the process, whose use may, or may not, be of relevance.

David Carson has already defined the aesthetic limits of graphic editing tools and the boundaries of the need for legibility. The response to all this post-punk industrial art became systematic and today it seems logical that years of tiny typographies in the middle of mega super-white spaces have given rise to a certain desire to scream. Lettering is not so much the result of public demand as a necessity for design and illustration professionals who sit down one afternoon with temperas after years of Freehand and find they have a great time. They may use Photoshop for the finishes, masks and shading, they may use graphics tablets; but the gesture of spontaneity is essential.

In the post-modern field of lettering today we could talk of a certain similarity in styles; not so much in the messages transmitted but in the tone. A certain carefreeness and a gung-ho attitude, which could almost be construed as revenge for so many hours spent in front of the computer.

Finally, it should also be added that even if it is a vindication on behalf of all that is "made by hand", the discipline is now global; it is taking place all over the world, wherever there are digital tools for graphic production. So why not come in and take a look?

Introducción

Sin establecer jerarquías, podríamos decir que el diseño gráfico está más cerca de la alfarería que de la pintura. Que diseñar una web está más cerca de arreglar un zapato que de concebir una ópera.

Esto parece haberlo comprendido muy bien una generación de diseñadores postmodernos que han superado la computadora. Han comprendido las limitaciones obvias del ordenador, que ha de dejado de ser un fin, un discurso en sí mismo, para convertirse una herramienta más del proceso, sin que su uso, o no, sea relevante.

David Carson ya definió los límites estéticos asumibles con herramientas de edición gráfica y los límites de la necesidad de una legibilidad. La respuesta a tanta plástica post-punk industrial se volvió uniformizadora y hoy parece lógico que después de años de tipografías diminutas en medio de mega-espacios super-blancos, haya ciertas ganas de gritar. El "lettering" no es tanto una demanda del público, es una necesidad de los profesionales del diseño y de la ilustración que, se ponen una tarde con unas témperas después de años de Freehand y descubren que se lo pasan pipa aún qué utilicen Photoshop para los acabados, máscaras y tramas, aún que utilicen tabletas gráficas, el gesto es importante y la espontaneidad necesaria. Hay un tono jocoso en todo esto del "lettering", un término aún carente de una buena definición y a la espera de una traducción: letras ilustradas o el arte de dibujar letras. También se puede hablar de cierta similitud de estilo, no tanto en los mensajes como en su tono.

Cierta despreocupación y una actitud gamberra que de alguna manera suena a venganza de las horas pasadas frente a los ordenadores. Y por último, añadir que aún que sea una reivindicación de lo "hecho a mano", esta disciplina es ya global, se está produciendo simultáneamente en todos los rincones del mundo donde hay herramientas digitales de producción gráfica. Pasen y vean.

Introduction

Sans vouloir établir des hiérarchies, nous pouvons dire que le design graphique est plus proche de la poterie que de la peinture. Concevoir une page web est plus proche de l'action d'arranger une chaussure que d'écrire un opéra.

Ces notions semblent être bien apprises par une génération de designers postmodernes qui sont allés plus loin que l'ordinateur. Ils ont assumé les limitations évidentes de l'informatique, qui n'est plus une fin, ni un discours en soi-même, mais elle devient un outil de plus du processus, sans que son usage, ou non, soit relevant.

David Carson définit les limites esthétiques avec des outils d'édition graphique et les limites du besoin d'une légitimité. La réponse à cette plastique post-punk industrielle devient formatrice et aujourd'hui, il est logique qu'après autant d'années de typographies minuscules au milieu de méga-espaces super-blancs, la volonté de crier apparaisse. Le "lettering" n'est pas une demande du public, il s'agit d'une nécessité des professionnels du design et de l'illustration qui, se réunissent une après-midi avec des aquarelles après des années de Freehand et qui découvrent qu'ils s'amusent, bien qu'ils soient obligés de recourir au Photoshop pour des finitions, des masques et des trames, ou qu'ils utilisent des tablettes graphiques. Le geste est important et la spontanéité devient essentielle. Il existe un ton cocasse dans tout le domaine du "lettering", une terminologie qui manque encore de définition et qui attend toujours une traduction: lettres illustrées ou l'art de dessiner des lettres. On peut parler de similitude de style, pas en ce qui concerne les messages mais plutôt le ton. L'insouciance et l'attitude dévoyée se décrivent d'un certain mode comme vengeance des heures passées face à l'ordinateur. Même s'il s'agit d'une revendication de ce qui est "fait à la main", cette discipline est déjà devenu globale, elle est produite simultanément dans tous les coins du monde où il existe des outils digitaux de production graphique. Regardez et jouissez !

Introduccione

Senza stabilire delle gerarchie, si potrebbe dire che il design grafico è più vicino all'arte della ceramica che alla pittura. Che progettare una pagina web è più simile alla riparazione di una scarpa che alla concezione di un'opera. Questo sembra averlo capito molto bene una generazione di designer postmoderni che hanno superato il computer. Hanno compreso i limiti evidenti del pc, che ha smesso di essere un fine, un discorso a sé stante, per convertirsi in un altro strumento in più del processo, senza che il suo uso, o no, sia rilevante. David Carson definì i limiti estetici asumibili con strumenti di edizione grafica ed i limiti della necessità di una leggibilità. La risposta a tanta plastica post-punk industriale diventò uniformizzante ed oggi sembra logico che dopo anni di tipografie minute in mezzo a mega-spazi super-bianchi, vi sia una certa voglia di gridare. Il "lettering" non nasce da una domanda del pubblico, ma dalla necessità dei professionisti del design e dell'illustrazione che, dopo anni di Freehand, si mettono a lavoro un pomeriggio con alcune tempere e scoprono che lo passano da sballo nonostante utilizzino Photoshop per le rifiniture, maschere e trame ed utilizzino tavolette grafiche: il gesto è importante e la spontaneità necessaria. C'è un tono giocoso nel "lettering", un termine ancora carente di una buona definizione e in attesa di una traduzione: lettere illustrate o arte del disegnare lettere. Si può parlare anche di una certa similitudine di stile, non tanto nei messaggi ma nel suo tono. Una certa spensieratezza ed un atteggiamento vandalico che in qualche modo suona a vendetta per le ore trascorse di fronte al computer. Infine si può aggiungere che nonostante sia una rivendicazione della cosa "fatta a mano", questa disciplina è già globale, si sta producendo simultaneamente in tutti gli angoli del mondo laddove ci sono strumenti digitali di produzione grafica.

Martín Allais

martin@togetheronemoretime.com
www.togetheronemoretime.com

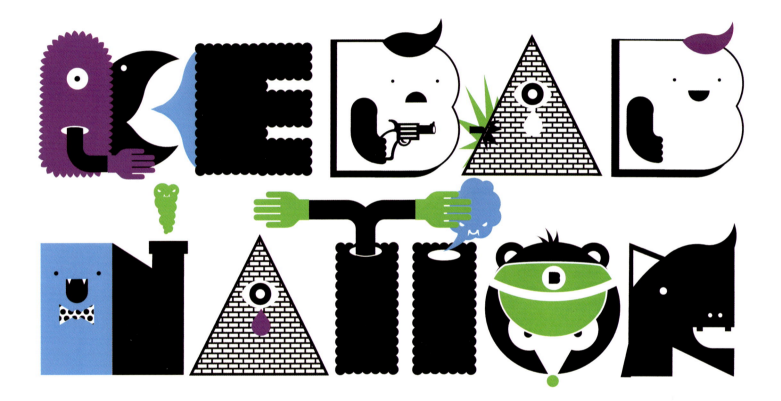

NEW AMSTERDAM

LESLIE BARLOW

Nick Radford

nick@frootful.co.uk
www.frootful.co.uk

what not to eat

UNLESS YOUR COMPANY'S GOT A WEEKEND SHIFT, THE ONLY POINT OF LEAVING MONITORS, PRINTERS, LIGHTS AND PHOTOCOPIERS SWITCHED ON AT FRIDAY HOME-TIME IS IF YOU'RE WASTING ENERGY FOR CHARITY.

or out of spite. or for a dare.

We all use 50% more water than we did 25 years ago. So are we 50% thirstier, 50% dirtier or 50% lazier?

Sveta Sebyakina

sebyakina@yahoo.com
www.sebyakina.ru

8:00

morning

8:00
восемь ноль ноль | авторский проект Светланы Себякиной

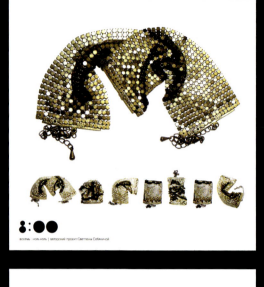

morning

8:00
восемь ноль ноль | авторский проект Светланы Себякиной

доброе утро

8:00
восемь ноль ноль | авторский проект Светланы Себякиной

morning

8:00
восемь ноль ноль | авторский проект Светланы Себякиной

доброе утро

8:00
восемь ноль ноль | авторский проект Светланы Себякиной

доброе утро

8:00
восемь ноль ноль | авторский проект Светланы Себякиной

morning

8:00

доброе утро

8:00

morning

8:00
восемь ноль ноль | авторский проект Светланы Себякиной

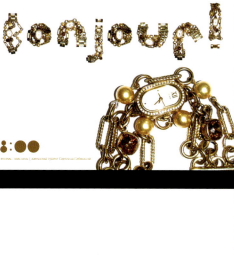

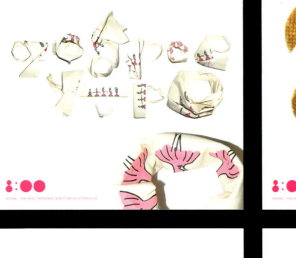

Andy Smith

andy@asmithillustration.com
www.asmithillustration.com

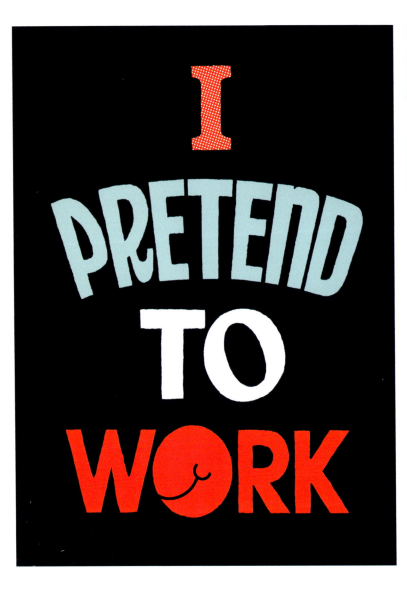

MICHEL CIMENT
NICOLAS KLOTZ
CATHERINE BREILLAT
JEAN-MICHEL FRODON
EUGENE GREEN
AGNES VARDA
LE CINEMA FRANÇAIS
THE LEGACY OF 68

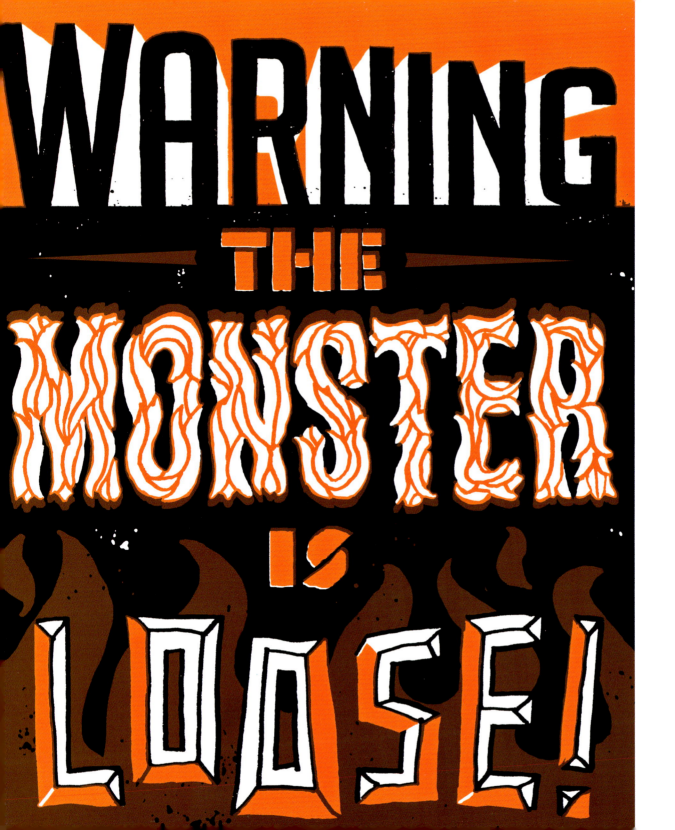

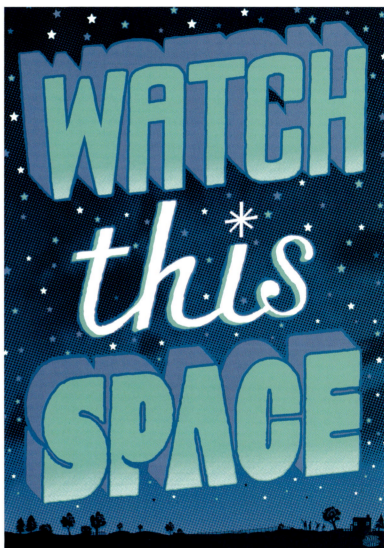

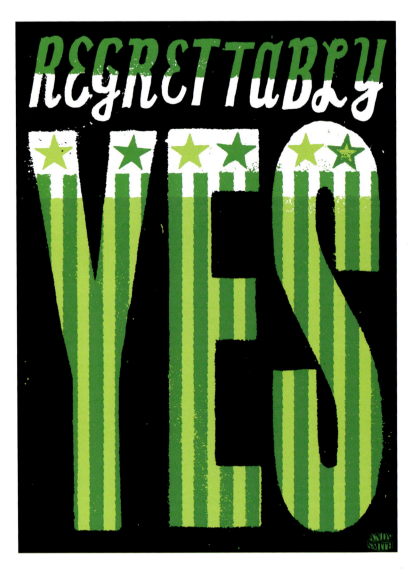

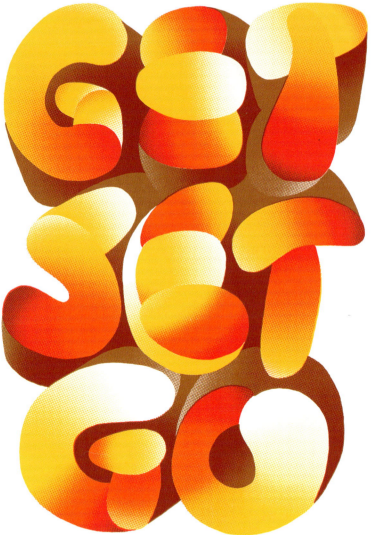

Simon Wild

mail@simonwild.com
www.simonwild.com

A TOE CAN REVEL
LEAVE NO TRACE
A TEN ACRE LOVE
CREATE A NOVEL

'he had **White** flame comin out his shoes'

Alberto Rodríguez

hola@stereoplastika.com
www.stereoplastika.com

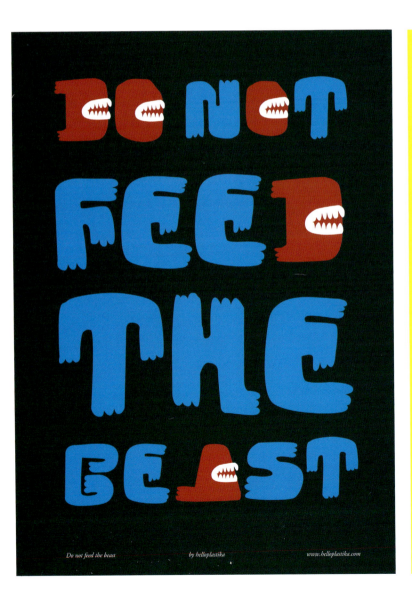

Do not feed the beast   by helloplastika   www.helloplastika.com

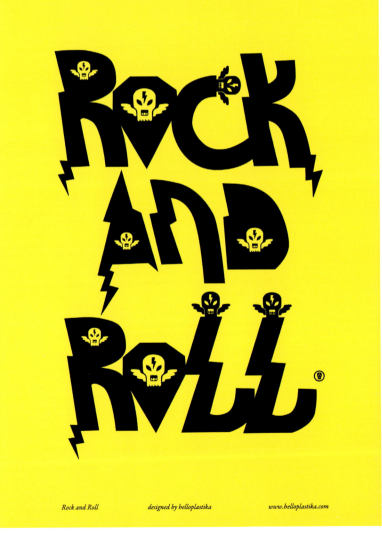

Rock and Roll   designed by helloplastika   www.helloplastika.com

Chris Bianchi

chris@chrisbianchi.co.uk
www.chrisbianchi.co.uk

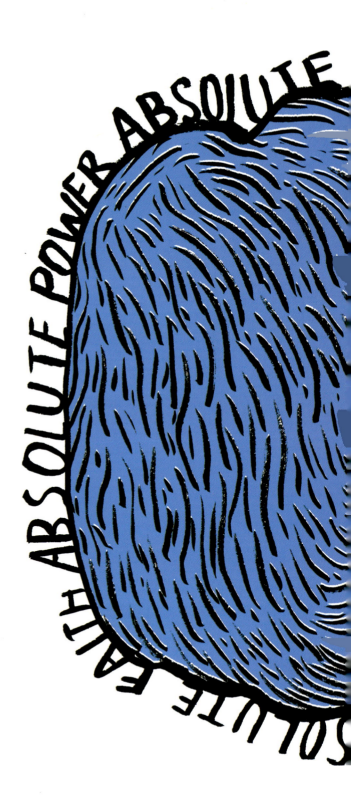

SON OF DAVE

PLUS SPECIAL GUEST

18 JUNE 2008

Roundhouse

STUDIO

CHALK FARM ROAD, CAMDEN, LONDON

WWW.ROUNDHOUSE.ORG.UK

BOX OFFICE ✆ 08448828008 ★ TICKETS : £12

WWW.MYSPACE.COM/THESONOFDAVE ☀ HTTP://SONOFDAVE.BLOGSPOT.COM

WWW.KARTEL.MU

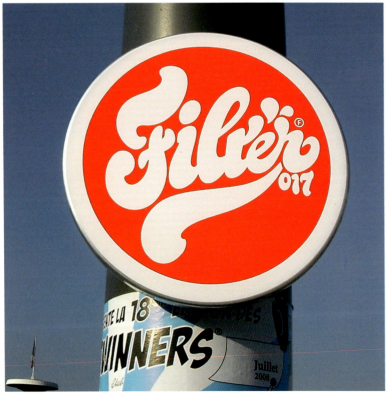

Polaroid Impulse
AutoFocus System

CHEESE!!!

UNITED GRAPHIC KINGDOM

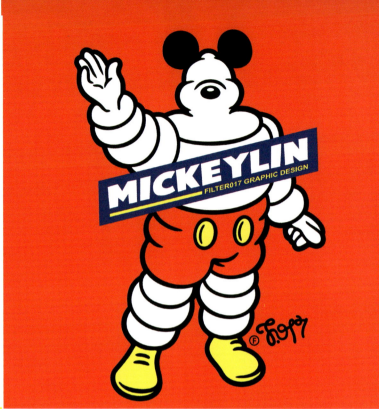

MICKEYLIN

FILTER017 GRAPHIC DESIGN

EVERYTHING GOES WELL! GUNG SI 發中 DUMPLINGS good luck!

REVERSE THE CURSE! GO!

MAY ALL YOUR WISHES COME TRUE. 福 PEACE ALL YEAR FATSAN

GREETING IN "OX"-YEAR!

Filter017® Graphic Design.

filter017.blogspot.com

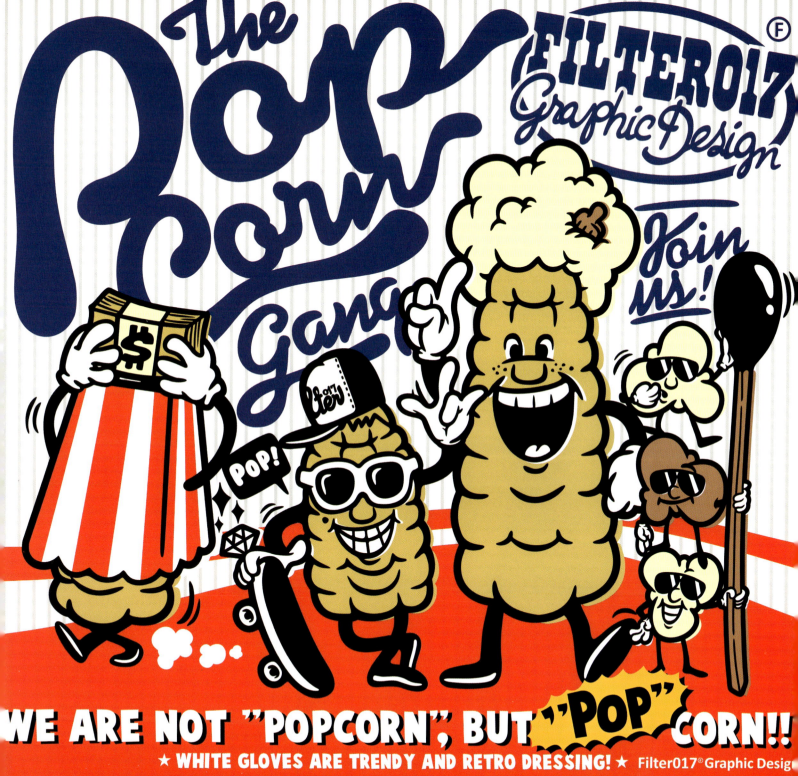

Jamie Tao

jamieetao@gmail.com
www.jamietao.com

Jugando en el mar,
en la arena,
viviendo faci

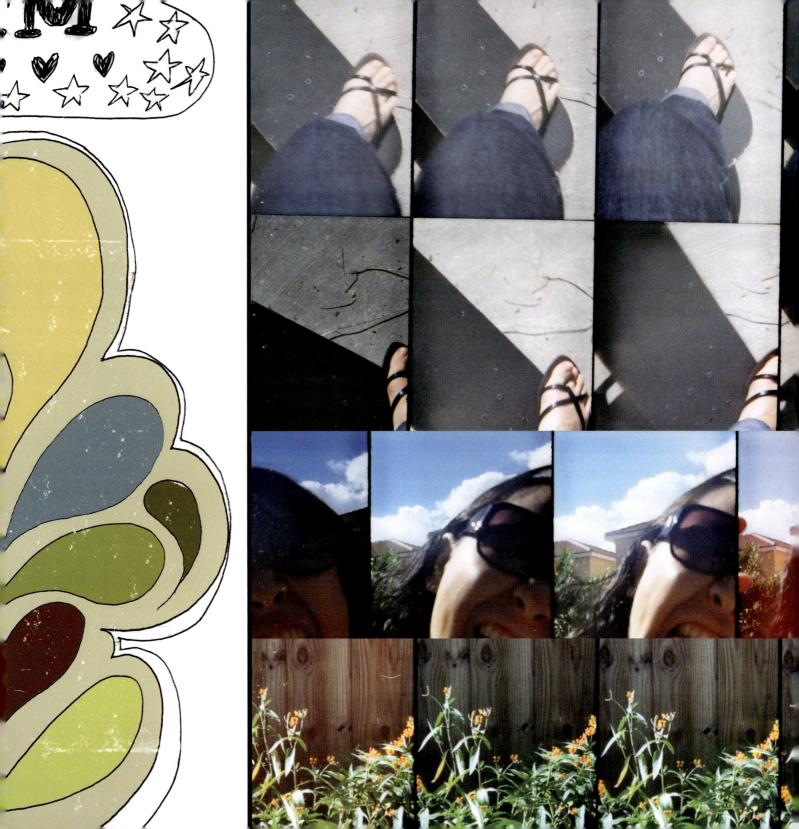

Raimond Chaves

rai@puiqui.com

DES DE NOVA YORK

ARCO Y FLECHA PRESENTA

MÚSICA RARA

AL MERCAT DE LES FLORS

San Miguel, donde está tu música

ELLERY ESKELIN
AMB ANDREA PARKINS
i JIM BLACK

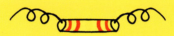

TIM BERNE
"SCIENCE FRICTION"

★ ★ ★

GIRA 10è ANIVERSARI

JESSICA CONSTABLE, VEU CONVIDADA
ESKELIN, SAXO TENOR
PARKINS, PIANO, ACORDIÓ I SÀMPLER
BLACK, BATERIA I PERCUSSIÓ

TIM BERNE, SAXOS ALT I BARÍTON
HERB ROBERTSON, TROMPETA
MARC DUCRET, GUITARRA ELÉCTRICA
CRAIG TABORN, TECLATS I ELECTRÒNICA
TOM RAINEY, BATERIA

30 DE NOVEMBRE
21:30H

4 DE DESEMBRE
21:30H

EL 3MEN DO

tomajazz

TEL·ENTRADA 902 10 12 12
CAIXA CATALUNYA telentrada.com

Ajuntament de Barcelona

Institut de cultura:

MERCAT DE LES FLORS

WWW.ARCOFLECHA.ES

ATENCIÓ: ESCOLTAR AMB MOLTA CURA

ARCO Y FLECHA Y
VAMPISOUL RECORDS
PRESENTAN EN VIVO

SABADO 9 DE
JULIO 2005
SALA ARENA
MADRID
23 HS

NUEVO CD
JOE BATAAN
CALL MY NAME
VAMPISOUL RECORDS

LATIN SOUL
FROM EL B

MARC RIBOT

Y LOS CUBANOS POSTIZOS

CELOFUNK 2

SABROSOS

Esther Aarts

hi@estadiezijn.nl
www.estadiezijn.nl

mister moustache

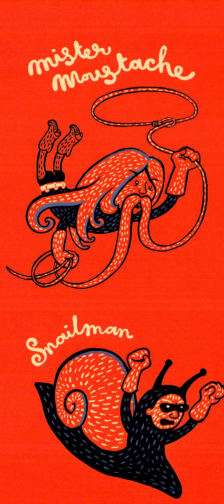

Infinite Cooper

lady lawnmower

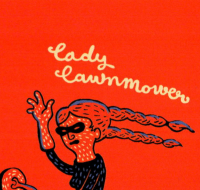

Snailman

the Scrubber

pointless man

airtriangle hero

the windscreen wiper

Captain Knäckebröd

miss Spellcheck

Chrissie Abbot

hello@chrissieabbott.co.uk
www.chrissieabbott.co.uk

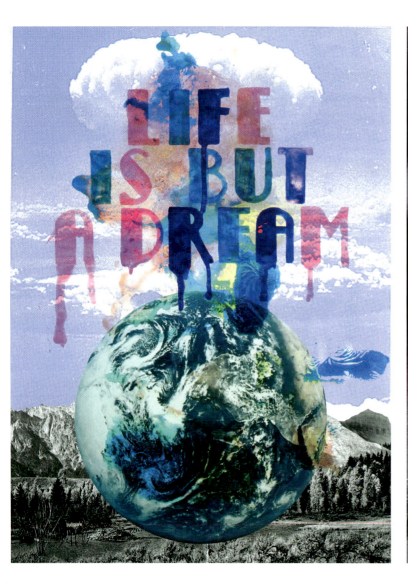

YOU LOOK GREAT WHEN I'M HIGH

MORE THAN REAL

Joel Lozano

joel@studiocopyright.com
www.joellozano.com

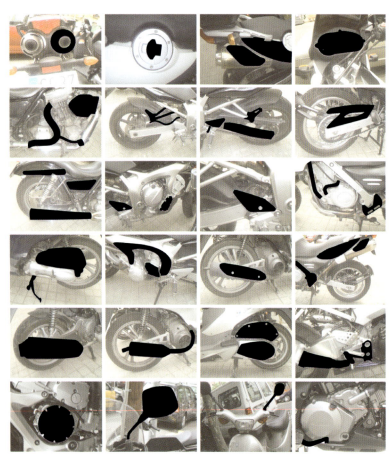

ABCDEFGHIJKLMNÑOPQRSTUVWXYZ◎123456789
abcdefghijklmnñopqrstuvwxyz◎123456789

TIPOGRAFÍA MODULAR

WORKSHOP CON ANDREU BALIUS

ABCaBC

ROBIN FRANK Y JOEL LOZANO

MOTO TYPE

COPYRIGHT FONTS

ABCDEFGHIJKLMNÑOPQRSTUVWXYZ0123456789

abcdefghijklmnñopqrstuvwxyz0123456789

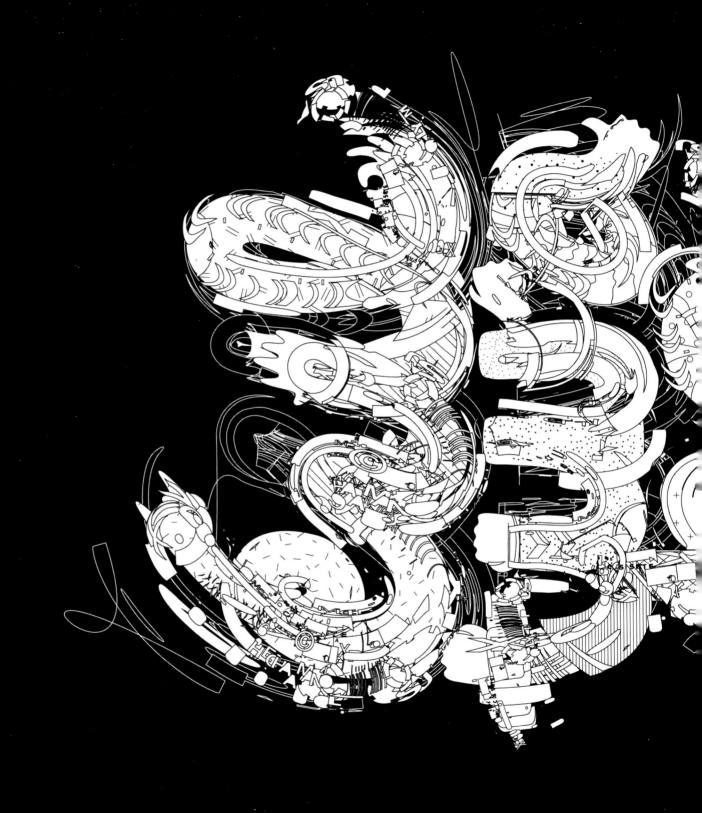

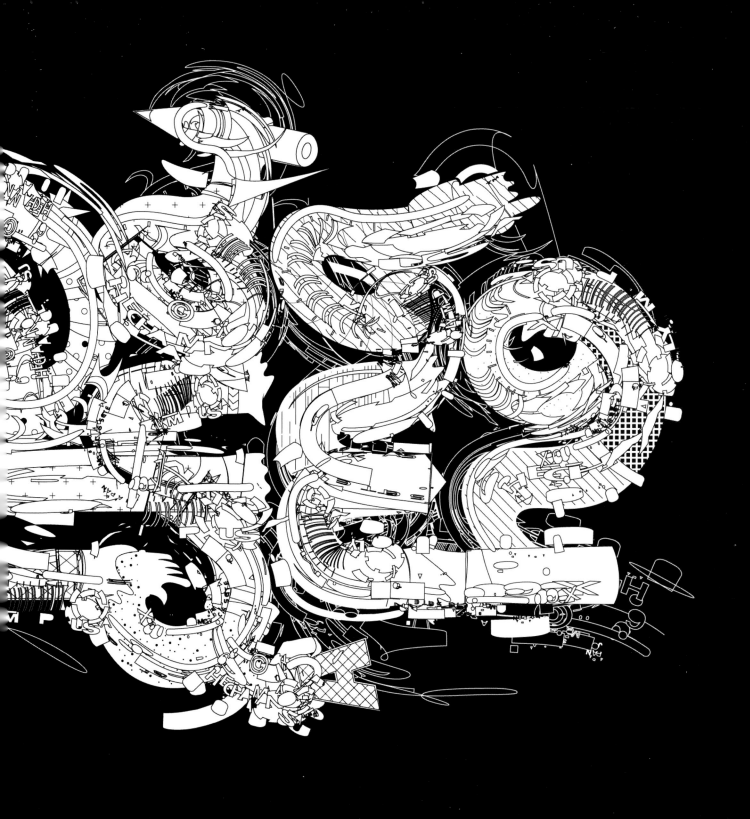

Andrés Yeah.

andresbfl@hotmail.com
www.yeahyeah.com.ar

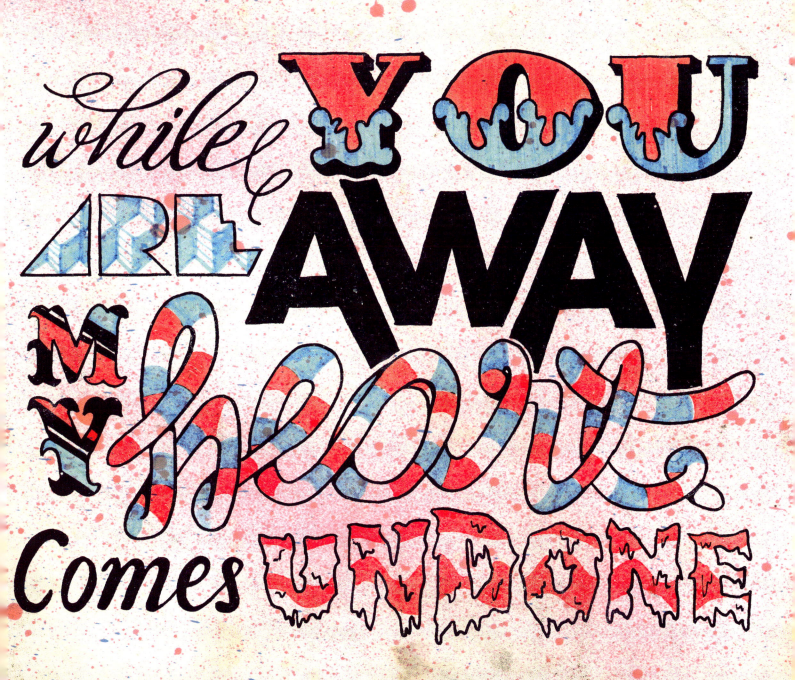

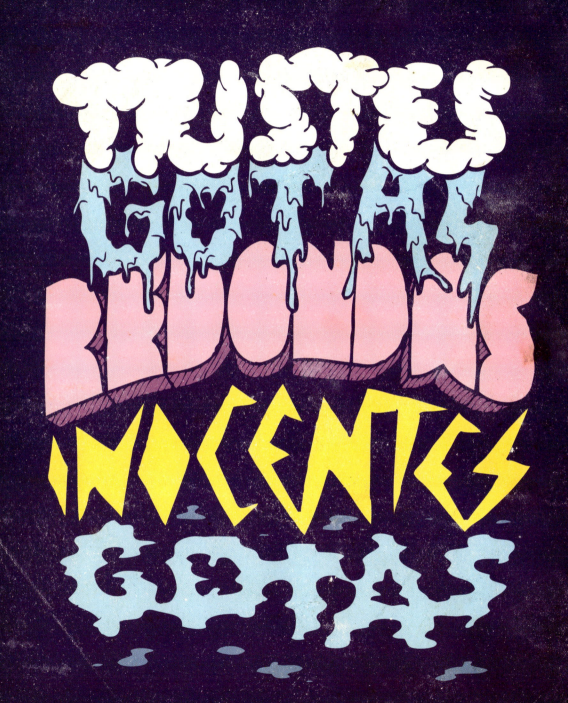

Andrea Posada

i@andreaposada.com
www.andreaposada.com

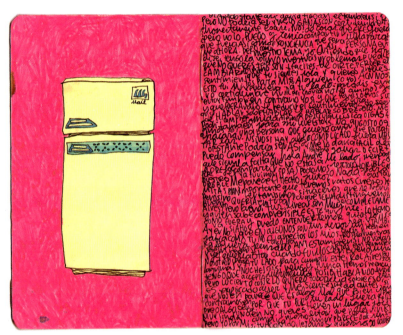

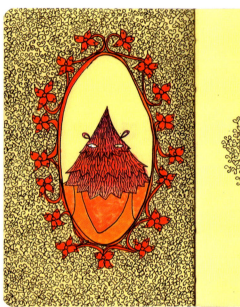

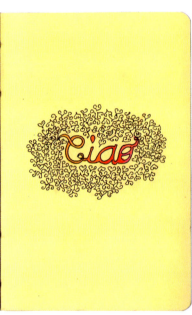

TU MADRE
MERCADO?
MATERIALES
ACOSTARZON
ACORDARL
UN SIMPLE TRISTE
HELP ME
PRIMAVERA
LAS MISMAS PALABRAS
PROPONIENDO
I DON'T THINK
ZORRO PEOPLE
DESEMPLEO
COMPRAMOS
BUENOS AIRES
UNA PELÍCULA
ESCULTURAS
PRESTARMELO
LA ORQUESTA
TOO MUCH
IMPROVISACIÓN
IMBECIL
LA VOLUNTAD
ENTERRÁNDOME EN LAS PALABRAS

Laura Varsky

lv@lauravarsky.com.ar
www.lauravarsky.com.ar

ESTAMOS INVITADOS A TOMAR EL TÉ. La tetera es de porcelana pero no se ve. La leche tiene frío y la abrigaré, le pondré un sobretodo mío largo hasta los pies. Cuidado cuando beban, se les va a caer la nariz dentro de la taza y eso no está bien. Detrás de una tostada se escondió la miel, la manteca muy enojada la retó en inglés. Mañana se lo llevan preso a un coronel por pinchar a la mermelada con un alfiler. Parece que el azúcar siempre negra fue y de un susto se puso blanca tal como la ven. Un plato timorato se casó anteayer a su esposa la cafetera la trata de usted. Los pobres coladores tienen mucha sed porque el agua se les escapa cada 2 por 3.

lau

canción de TOMAR EL TÉ
de María Elena Walsh

84

IT'S LIKE A RAINBOW SOMING THE COLORS IN THE AIR EVERYWHERE

BUSCO
NO ES UN SI UN
VERBO NO VERTIS
NO INDICA ACCION
QUIERE DECIR TRAS ALGUIEN YACER PORQUE
NO SI RA SINO ALGUIEN NO
ENCU TIENE
ENTRO

86

For 3 months (they had been married in April) they lived in a special kind of bliss. She passed the autumn in a strange love nest. It is not strange that she grew thin. She had a light attack, after that → her health never returned. Finally one afternoon she was able to into the garden. This was the last day she was well enough to be up. To be the doctors saw a diminishing life, a life gliding away, absolutely without their knowing why. The illness never worsened during the daytime, but each morning she awakened pale as → death, almost in a swoon. Finally she died. The servant, when she came in afterward to strip the now empty bed, stared wonderingly for a moment at the pillow. "Sir!" she said in a low voice. "There are stains on the pillow that look like blood." Immediately dropped it. "It's very heavy" the servant whispered trembling. He ripped open the case and the ticking with a slash. In the bottom of the pillow case, among the feathers slowly moving its hairy legs, was a monstrous animal, a living, viscous ball. Night after night, this abomination had stealthily applied its to the girl's temples, sucking her blood. In 5 days, in 5 nights, the monster had drained her life away.

FROM "EL ALMOHADÓN DE PLUMAS" BY HORACIO QUIROGA.

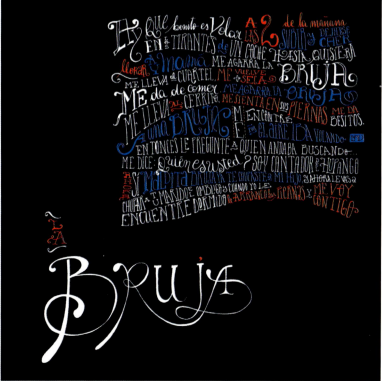

Rodrigo Francisco

typefunk@gmail.com
www.behance.net/sjalv

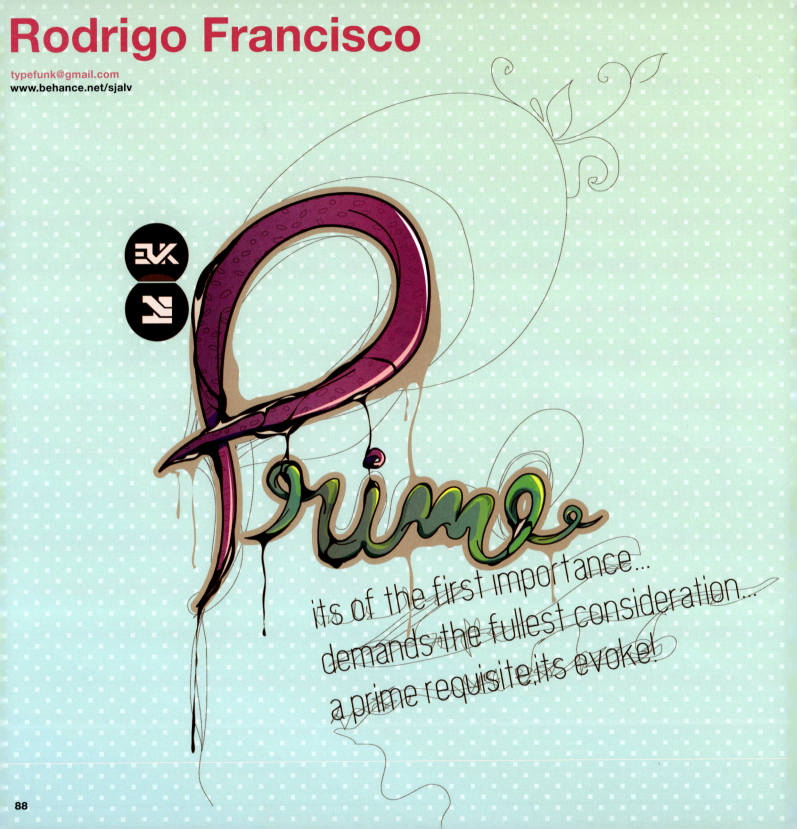

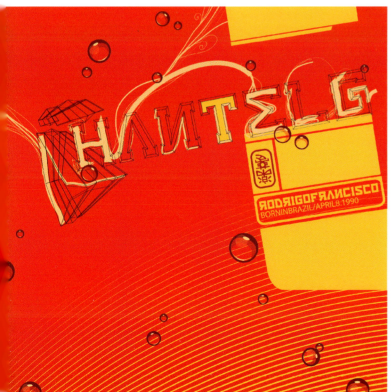

Ekaterina Erschowa

info@meetmetwice.com
www.meetmetwice.com

OUR SOCIAL RESPONSIBILITY IS AT THE HEART OF WHAT WE DO

Alison Richards

ali@alisonrichards.net
www.alisonrichards.net

Sophie Henson

info@synergyart.co.uk
www.sophiehenson.com

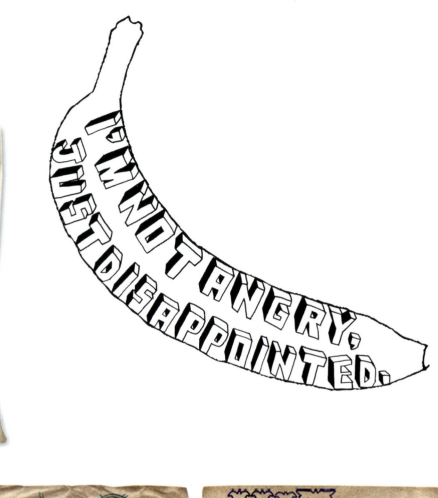

I'M NOT ANGRY,
JUST DISAPPOINTED.

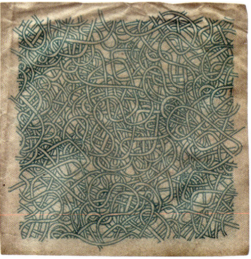

HIT ME BABY ONE MORE TIIME.

Roger Adam

claude@claudedieterich.com
www.behance.net/RogerAdam

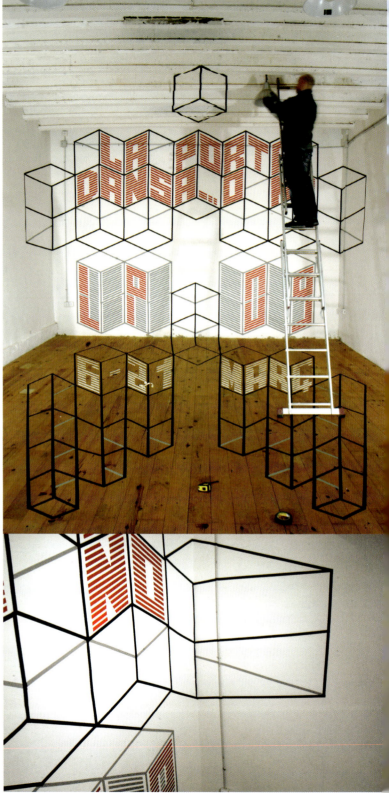

Claude Dieteirch

claude@claudedieterich.com
www.claudedieterich.com

Letters are simbols which turn matter into spirit

Las letras son simbolos que transforman la materia en espiritu

LAMARTINE

Las letras son símbolos que transforman la materia en espíritu

Les lettres
sont
des symboles
qui
transforment
la matière
en
esprit

Camelia Dobrin.

talktome@camellie.com
www.camellie.com

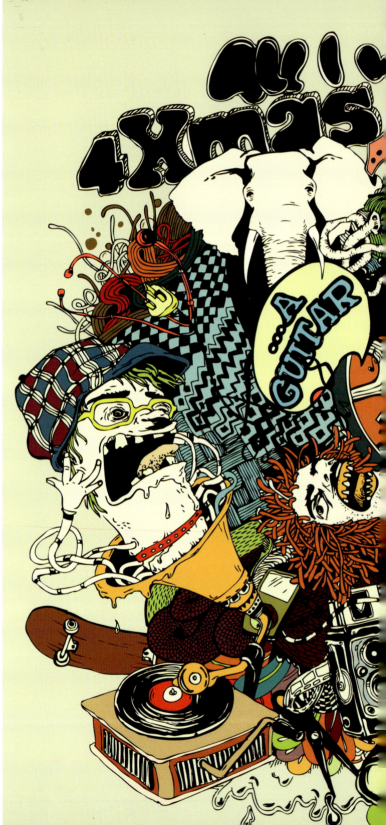

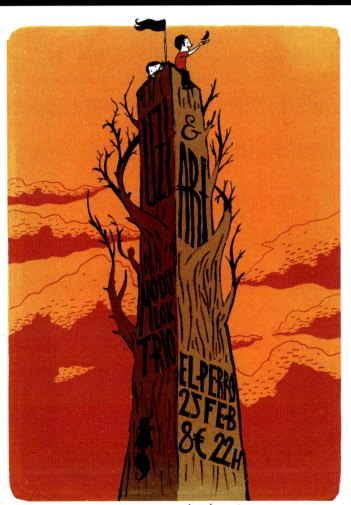

UZI & ARI (www.myspace.com/benshepard) + MODULOK TRIO (www.myspace.com/moduloktrio)
25 DE FEBRERO / 21:30H / 8€/ EL PERRO CLUB (C/PUEBLA 15)
ORGANIZA: SDEROCK (www.myspace.com/sderock)
DISEÑO: ABEL CUEVAS (www.flickr.com/photos/frankie_teardrop)

Giradiscos presenta:
SIMON FINN
+ The Missing Leech
La Casa de los Jacintos ~ 27 de septiembre ~ 22h ~ 8€
www.myspace.com/giradiscos

diseño:abel cuevas

SIX ORGANS OF ADMITTANCE / WOODEN SHJIPS

5 DE NOVIEMBRE / CLUB SAVOY / 21:30 11€/15€
ANTICIPADA: GIJON(PARADISO, SAVOY) OVIEDO(EL ÚLTIMO MONO)

HAWKWIND HACKSAW — YO LO HE VISTO TODO, LA VI EL MUNDO

diseño: abel cuevas

SALÓN de ACTOS del ATENEO de MADRID
23 de JUNIO · 22h · 2€
www.myspace.com/ATENEODEMADRID

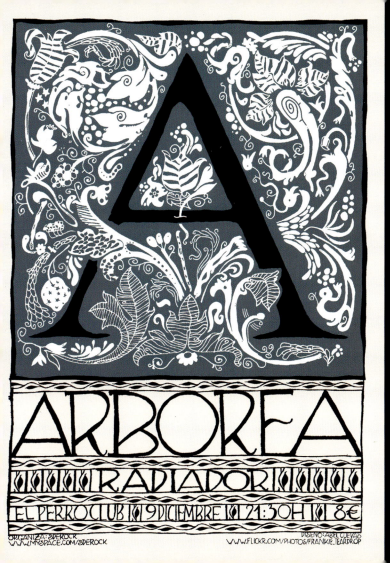

ARBOREA

XXXXX RADIADOR XXXXX

EL PERRO CLUB X 9 DICIEMBRE X 21:30H X 8€

ORGANIZA: SDEROCK
WWW.MYSPACE.COM/SDEROCK

DISEÑO: ABEL CUEVAS
WWW.FLICKR.COM/PHOTOS/FRANKIE_TEARDROP

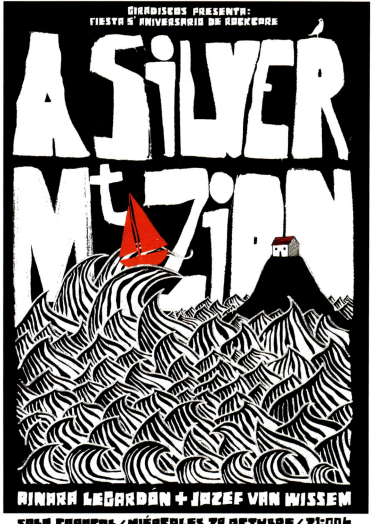

GIRADISCOS PRESENTA:
FIESTA 5° ANIVERSARIO DE ROCKCORE

A SILVER Mt ZION

AINARA LEGARDÓN + JOZEF VAN WISSEM

SALA CARACOL / MIÉRCOLES 29 OCTUBRE / 21:00h
15 € ANTICIPADA (EN MELOCOTÓN) / 18 € TAQUILLA

NICK CASTRO & THE YOUNG ELDERS + DEN
27 DE ENERO / 21:30H / PICNIC (C/MINAS 1) /8E
ORGANIZA: QUESOPANTALONES
(www.myspace.com/quesopantalones)

HELLO CUCA DJs
+ LADYFEST SOUNDSYSTEM

22 ENERO 22:30
QK BAR C/PEZ 40

diseño: abel cuevas

GIRADISCOS PRESENTA:

SHARRON
KRAUS

NARCOLEPTICA

MARTES 24 FEBRERO/22:00/8 EUROS
EL PERRO CLUB (C/PUEBLA 15)

diseño: abel cuevas

Gemma Correll

gemmacorrell@hotmail.com
www.gemmacorrell.com

13

DAY 1

για η Αγγλία!

A LONG DAY'S TRAVELS

3.55 am BUS (1 SLEEP)

HANDY TRAVEL PILLOW

6.50. STANSTED AIRPORT

← I'M COLD

COOKIES

MY MOCHA TASTES OF NOTHING.
Hot Nothing.

COSTA

EYE TWITCHING SLIGHTLY

PROB. TOO MUCH COFFEE

ANTHONY'S MAN BAG 'O' SWEETS

OUR FRIENDLY BARISTO →

Delicious Drinks

HSBC

STOP

OTE

ο Λονδίνο. η Αγγλία

Είμαι στο αεροδρόμιο

η Αθήνα

BAD DRAWING OF A PLANE

FRAPPÉ

FIRST TIROPITTES ARE POLI OREO !!

♡ Η ΤΙΡΟΠΙΤΤΕΣ

10.25 ON THE PLANE

AEGEAN

4.33 we're ~~here~~ at Athens

7.15 NEARLY TIME TO BOARD OUR PLANE TO CRETE...

IT'S HOT!

→ I'm happy

Χανιά

DAY NINE

OUR LAST DAY IN CRETE

IN THE POOL

MMM, WARM...

THIS TIME TOMORROW I'LL BE VERY COLD ...

YOU MUST APPRECIATE THIS FEELING ...

"QUALITY" GIFTS FOR THE FOLKS BACK HOME

ΜΕΛΙ

OUZO

RAKI

¡HOLA!
Eakis Proobas

SOAP

TRYING TO EAT ALL THE LEFTOVER FOOD →

κυματιστά πατατάκια

↑ ANTHONY'S FLOTATION DEVICES ↑

Vanila BCN

hello@vanilabcn.com
www.vanilabcn.com

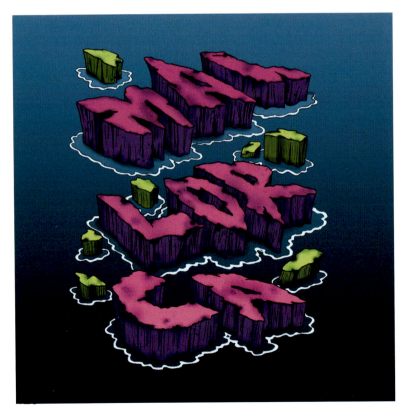

Syomic

syomik_tut@mail.ru
www.behance.net/syomik

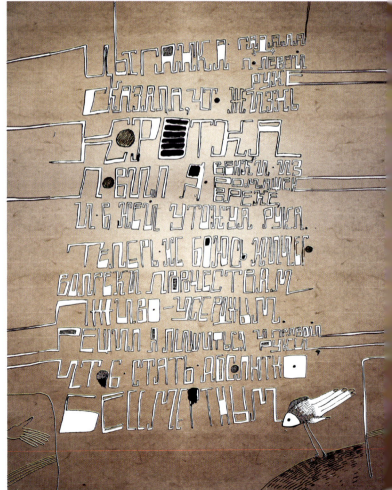

МНЕ ПОНАДОБИТСЯ
ОТВЁРТКА, МЕЛЬ-
ХИТРОВЫЕ ЛОЖК
И КРОТОВЬЯ ШКУР
ДРЫГ ДРЫГ
ШАРК ШАРК
ВИЛЬ ВИЛЬ

Alessandro Maida

scarful@gmail.com
www.scarful.com

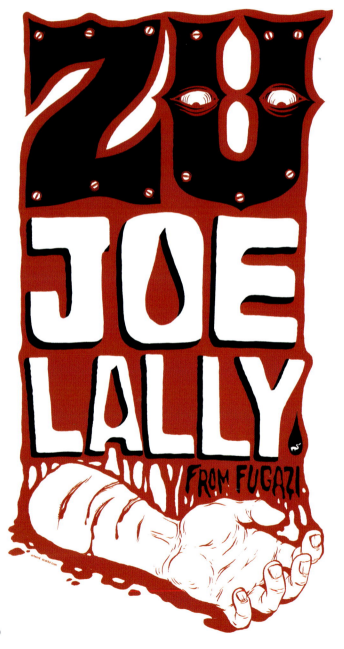

ZU & NOBUKAZU TAKEMURA

IDENTIFICATION WITH THE ENEMY:
"A KEY TO THE UNDERWORLD"

. ALONE WITH THE ALONE
THE CULPRIT
STANDING ON ZERO
THIS SPOT
NEW BUDDHAS IN STOCK
USUAL CONVERSATIONS
WITH YAMA
I'M NEXT FROM
AWAKE THE
EVERYONE GETS HIS OWN
HIS NEMESIS
DELIVER ME FROM
THE BOOK OF SELF.

MALUS TRACKS:
1) PSYCHOPOMP
2) HECATE, A RUMINATION
3) WE ARE ALL RETURNING

BONUS TRACKS MASTERED BY REEKS AT HOMBRELOBO / ROME.

133

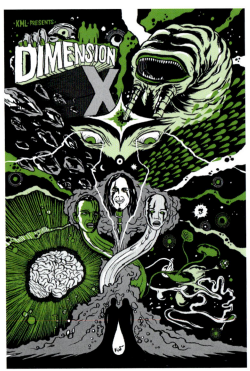

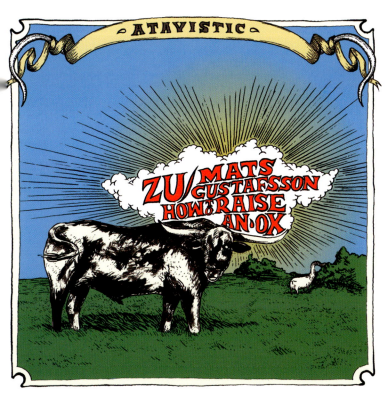

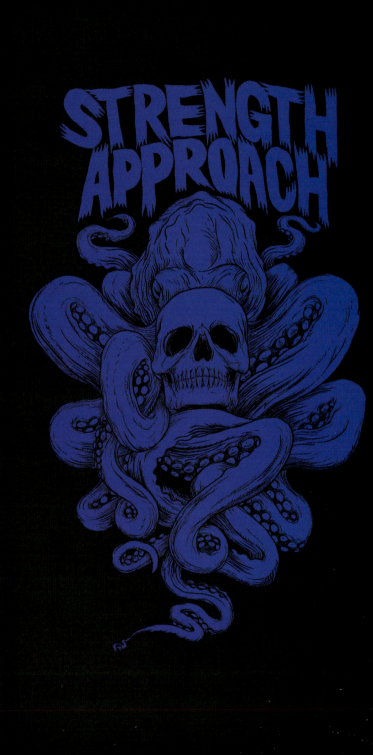

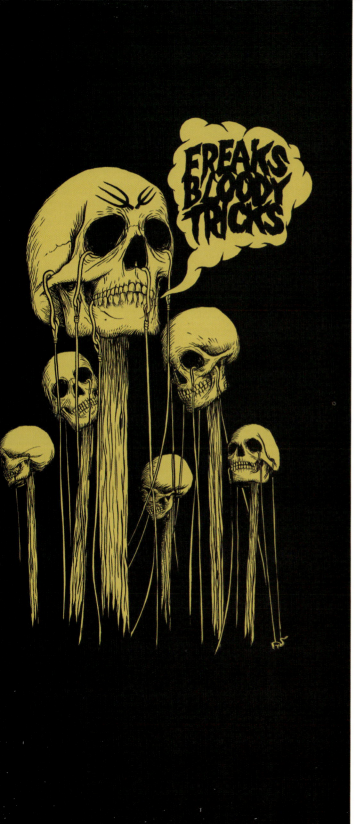

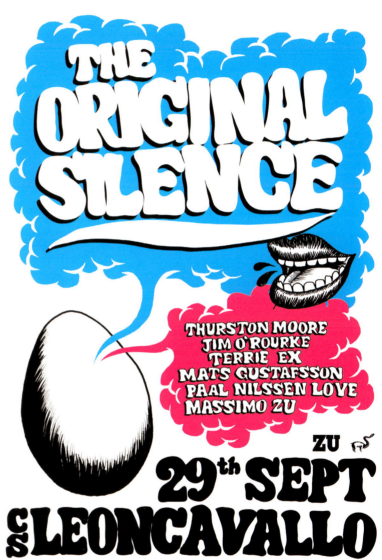

FREAKS BLOODY TRICKS

THE ORIGINAL SILENCE

THURSTON MOORE
JIM O'ROURKE
TERRIE EX
MATS GUSTAFSSON
PAAL NILSSEN LOVE
MASSIMO ZU

ZU
29th SEPT
CS LEONCAVALLO

137

Pedro Oliveira

hello@partidoalto.net
www.flickr.com/photos/pedroliveira

un joli garçon

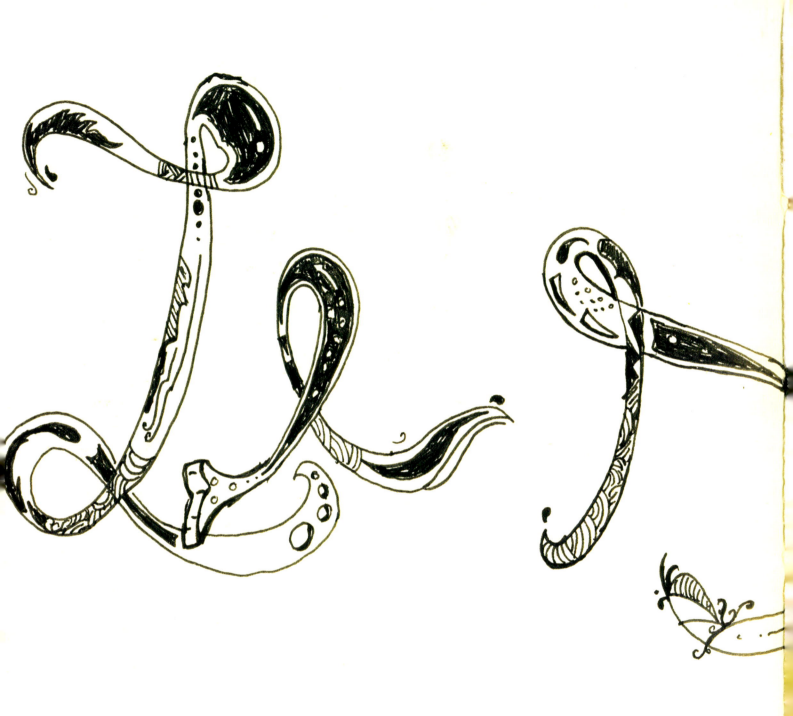

Nate Williams

art@magnetreps.com
www.n8w.com

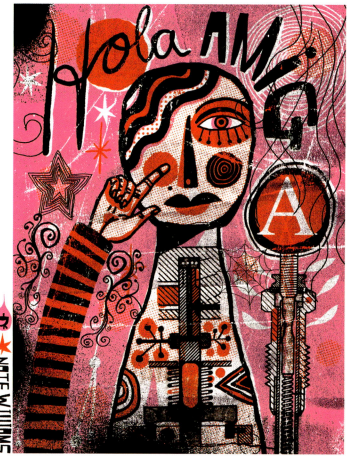

NATE WILLIAMS

JesseHora

jesse@jessehora.com
www.jessehora.com

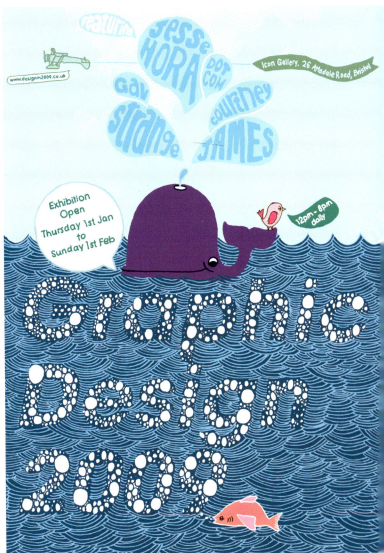

NO.2 type

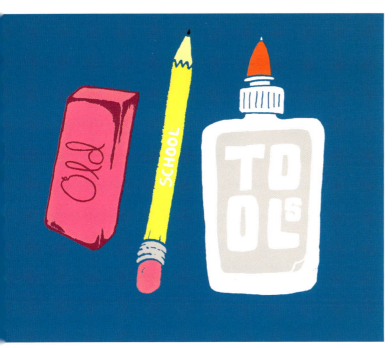

This is the

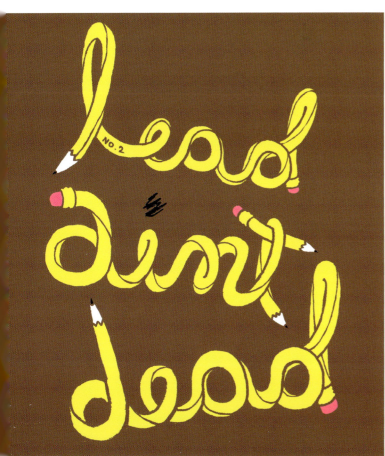

Jeff Finley

jeff@gomedia.us
www.jefffinley.org

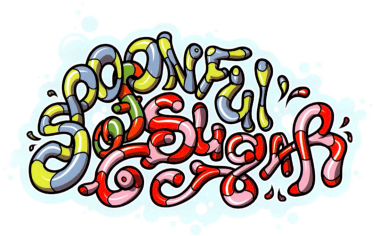

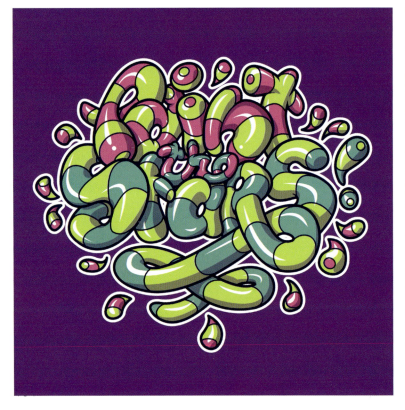

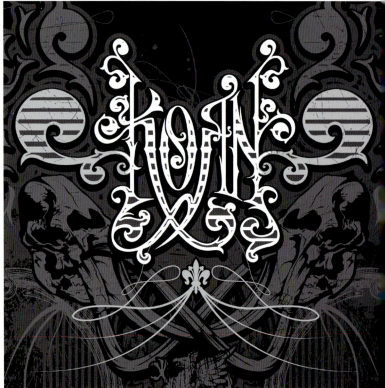

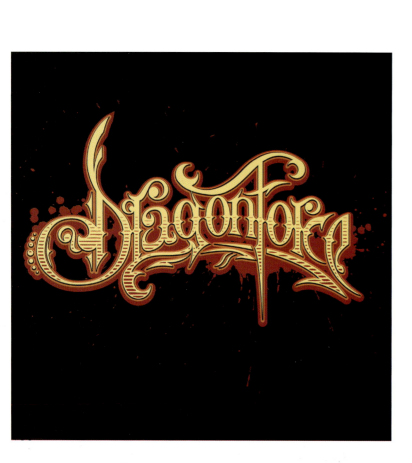

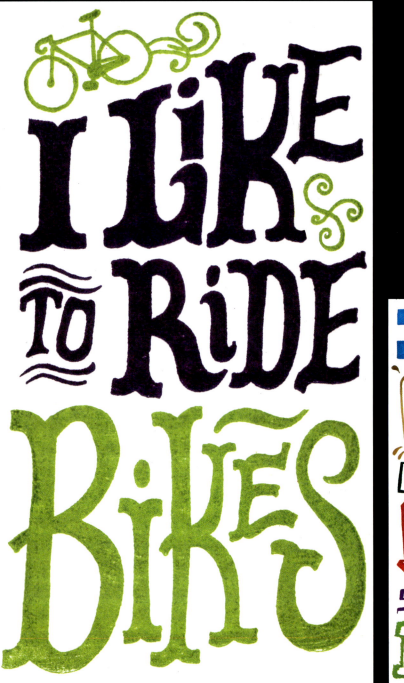

I LIKE TO RIDE BIKES

IF for ANY REASON YOU ARE NOT GOING to RETURN this CHURCH PRAYER RUG THEN this SACRED prophecy MUST BE DESTROYED

AND we've ONLY JUST BegUN.

the INTER-NET DOES NOT LOVE YOU.

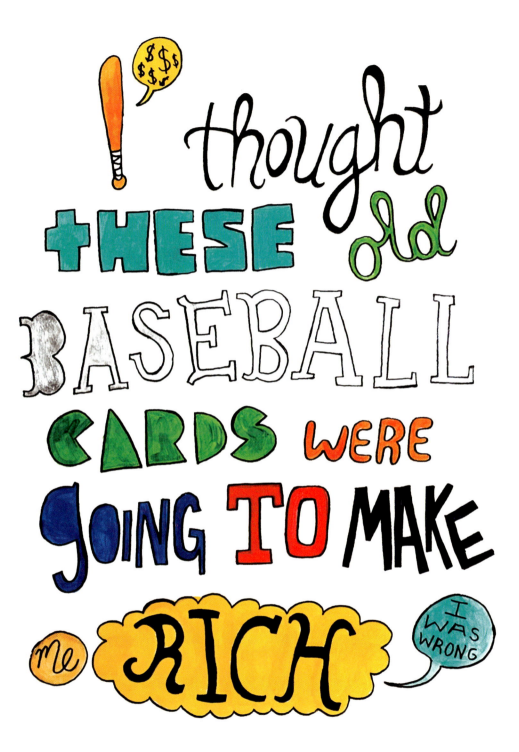

psycho 78, TWELVE O'CLOCK, DON'T BE LATE ALL THIS HORROR BUSINESS

The SOFT-MINDED MAN ALWAYS FEARS CHANE
MLK

LA LA LA LA LA LA LA LA LA LA
I HAD a dream
HA HA HA HA HA HA HA I HA HA HA HA HA
COULD BUY my WAY TO heaven WHEN I WOKE
I spent THAT ON A necklace.
K. West

Michelle Bowers

michellebowers@mac.com
www.michellebowers.com

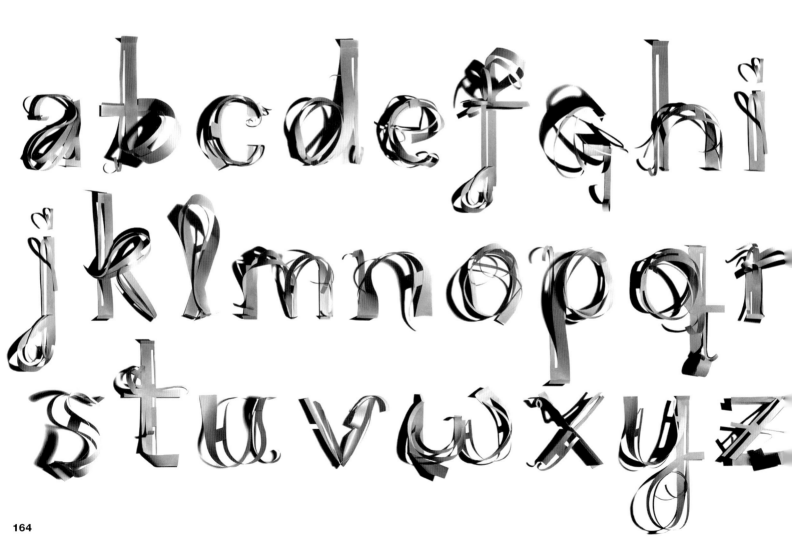

NATIONAL PORTFOLIO DAY

GRAND RAPIDS MI

NOVEMBER 1ST

NPDA
www.portfolioday.net

SATURDAY, NOVEMBER 1, 2008 Noon – 4pm
National Portfolio Day is an opportunity to meet with representatives from institutions offering visual arts professional programs accredited by the National Association of Schools of Art and Design. Over twenty five of the nation's leading art and design colleges and universities will review your artwork, discuss your educational and professional goals, and share information on art programs, careers, admissions, and financial aid. Bring your portfolio, parents, teachers, and friends.
FREE AND OPEN TO THE PUBLIC.

Hosted by Kendall College of Art and Design of Ferris State University

else, I change because I don't want to repeat myself. I don't find any particular joy in doing what I have already done before. I produce my best work when I'm really fascinated by what I'm doing. Now, the parameters within which I work can be very tight or they can be very large. Sometimes you are allowed to express yourself a lot more fully and other times you are expressing one particular thing for one particular reason. I don't have any particular problem with working in the way that I work at the moment with people like John Galliano at Dior. I understand at the end of the day that I have got to make another million billion whatever dollars it is for the company. I understand that and for better or for worse that is what I try and do.

THE N†H ENG

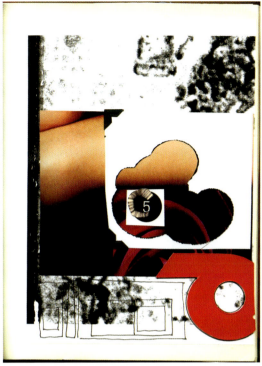

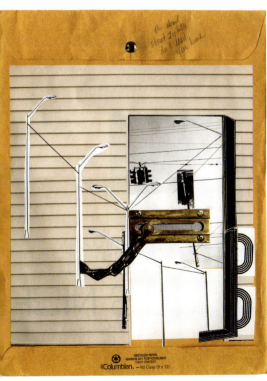

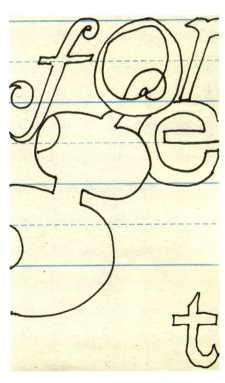

Lisa Rienermann

yeah@lisarienermann.com
www.lisarienermann.com

was ihr wollt

platz für lieblingsessen

erinnert ihr euch noch daran,

was ihr am liebsten gegessen habt, als ihr hungrig aus der schule kamt

oder was eure oma, mama oder euer papa für euch gekocht haben,

wenn ihr euch was wünschen konntet

hier sind eure top 7 von früher

1. fischstäbchen mit rahmspinat und bratkartoffeln

2. spaghetti bolognese

3. milchreis mit kirschen

4. gemüsesuppe mit apfelpfannekuchenplätzchen

5. kuchenteig

6. alles von der oma

7. kartoffelklöße mit sauerbraten

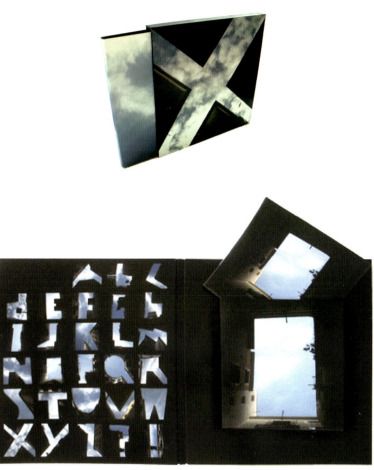

bfreemire@gmail.com
www.behance.net/GlobalAmusement

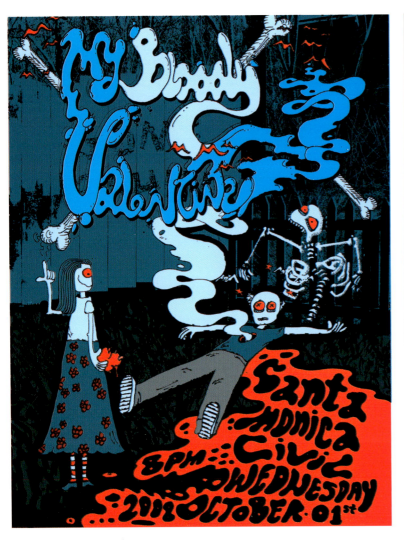

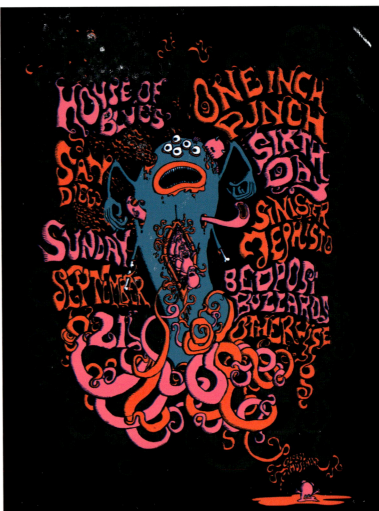

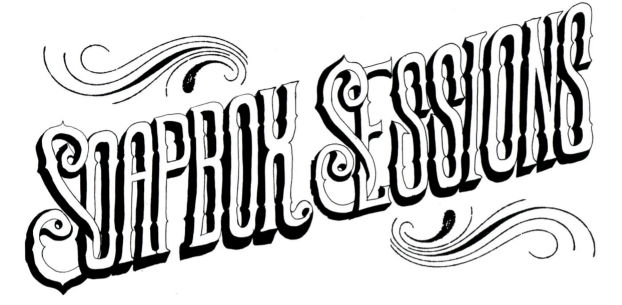

Julia Sonmi Heglund

julia@sonmisonmi.com
www.sonmisonmi.com

Coqué Azcona

coqueazcona@hotmail.com
www.coqueazcona.blogspot.com

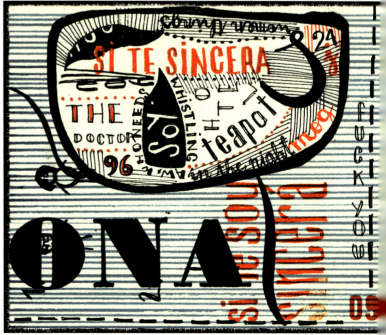

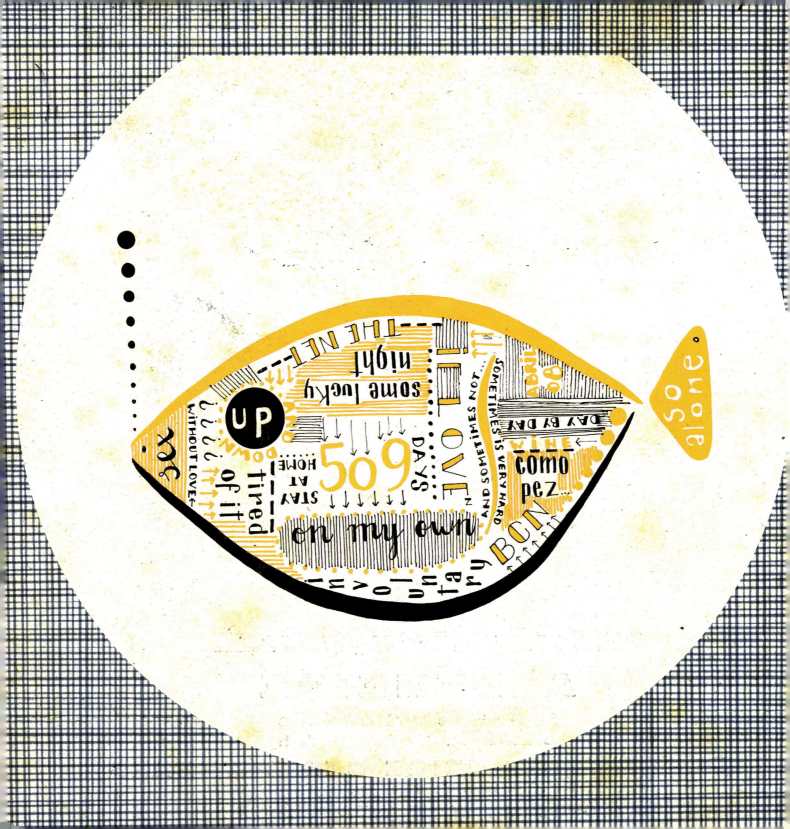

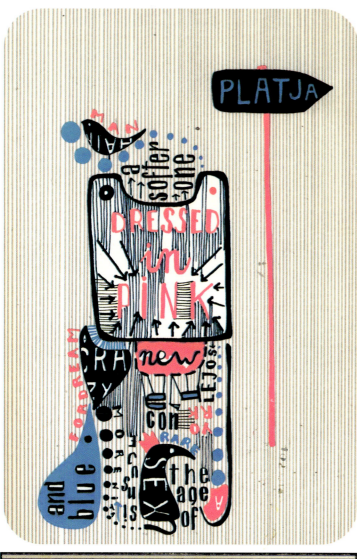

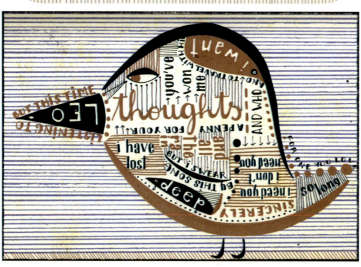

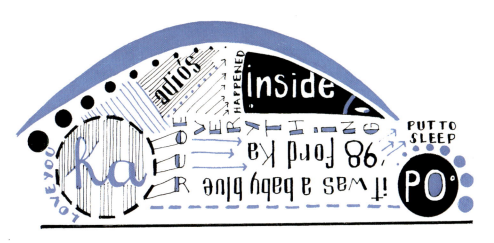

Martín Romero

martunderboy@gmail.com
www.martinromero.es

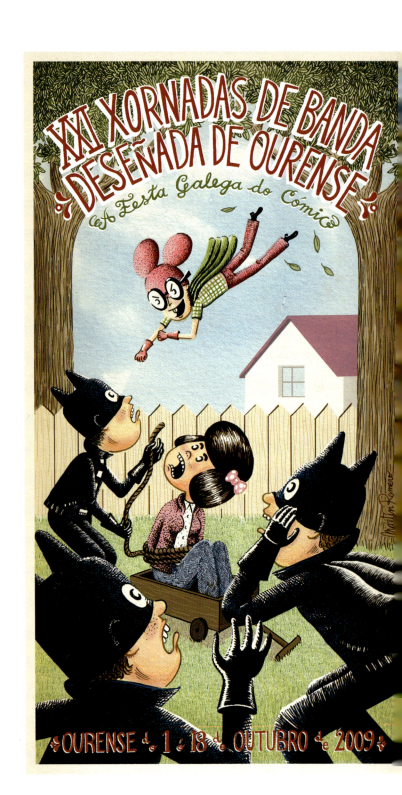

Joaquim Massana/Juanjo Saénz

quim@petitcomite.net
martunderboy@gmail.com

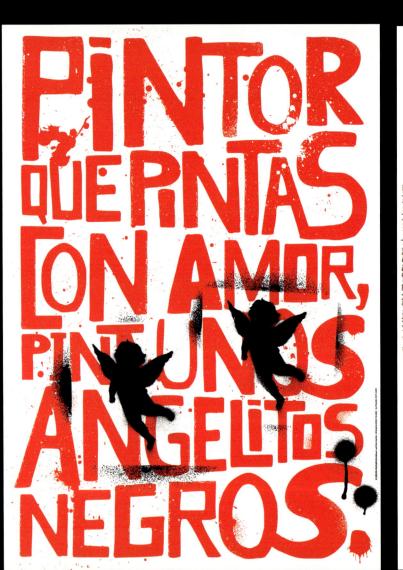

Jorge Parras

donjorgeparras@gmail.com
www.purebasure.com/jorgeparras

Keetra Dean Dixon

keetra@fromkeetra.com
www.fromkeetra.com

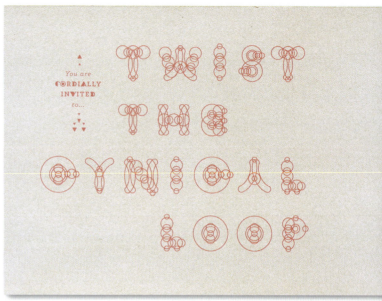

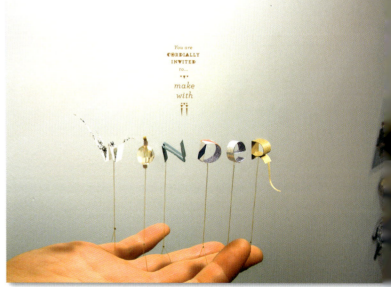

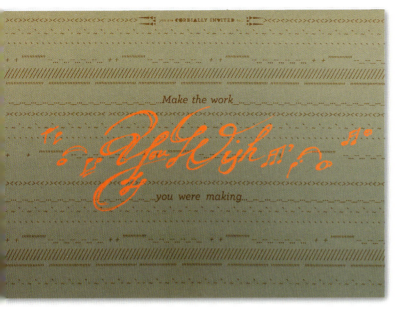

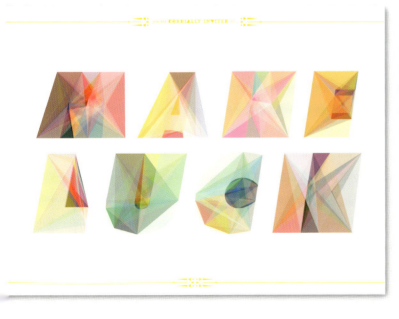

Karl Kwasny

karl@monaux.com
www.monaux.com

Jon Contino

joncontino@gmail.com
www.joncontino.com

THE
BROKLYN
CIRCUS

Please join us
As we celebrate
Erin & Jon's
Engagement

Bad Luck

Hit, Steal & Run

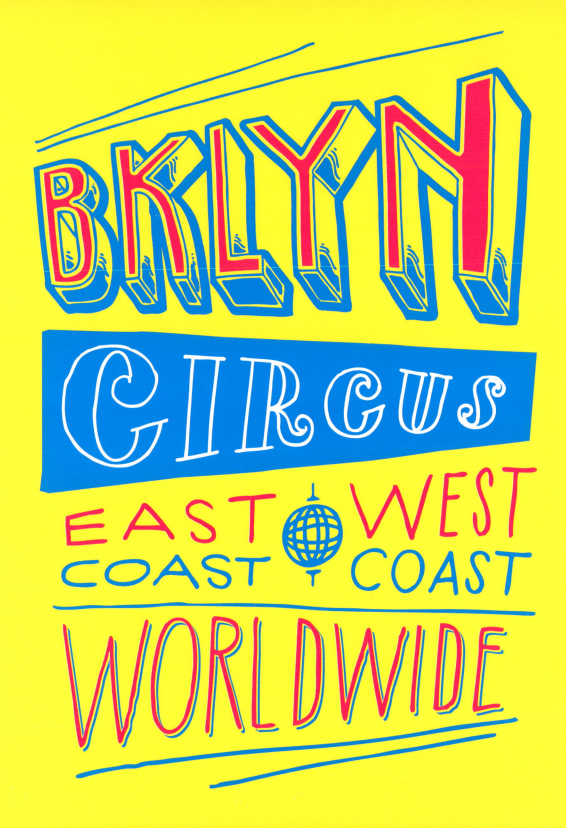

Francisco Martins

francisco@franciscomartins.com
www.franciscomartins.com

Reviverde
daGroselha
Velvet
MarianaTur

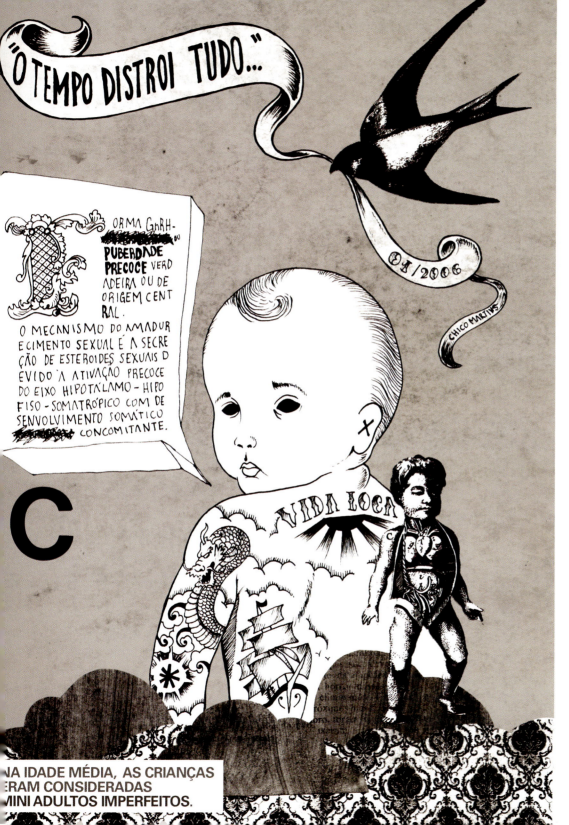

Nils Blishen

bascofive@gmail.com
www.bascofive.com

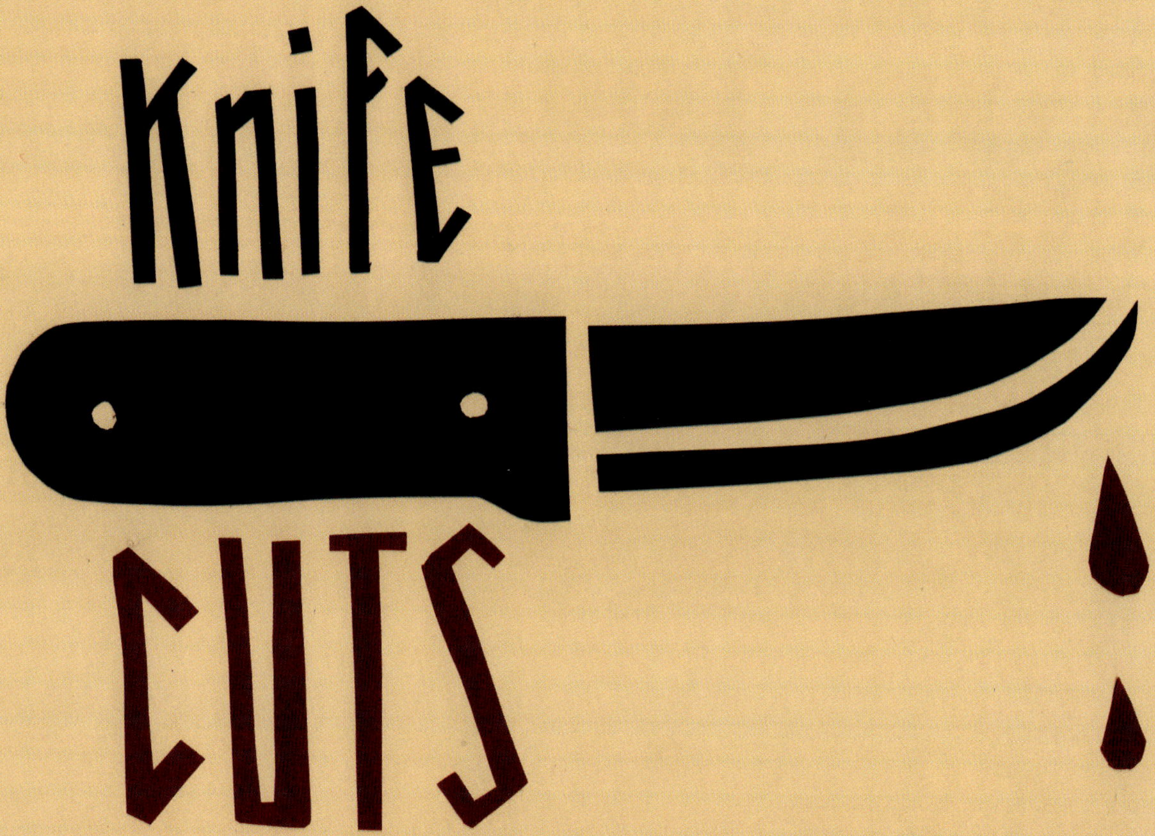
Knife
CUTS

Kyle and Khol PRESENTS

Mothra (Victoria)
Fun 100
Sticks (ex hand)
ok Vancouver ok

Sat
July 30
Pat's Pub 403 E Hastings Early Show
9:30
$5

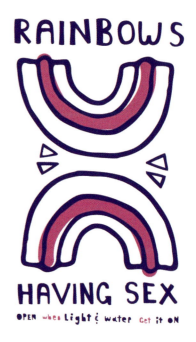

RAINBOWS

HAVING SEX

OPEN when Light & Water Get it ON

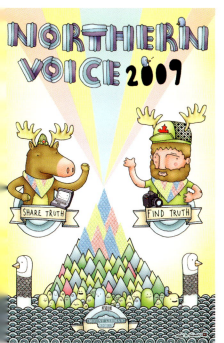

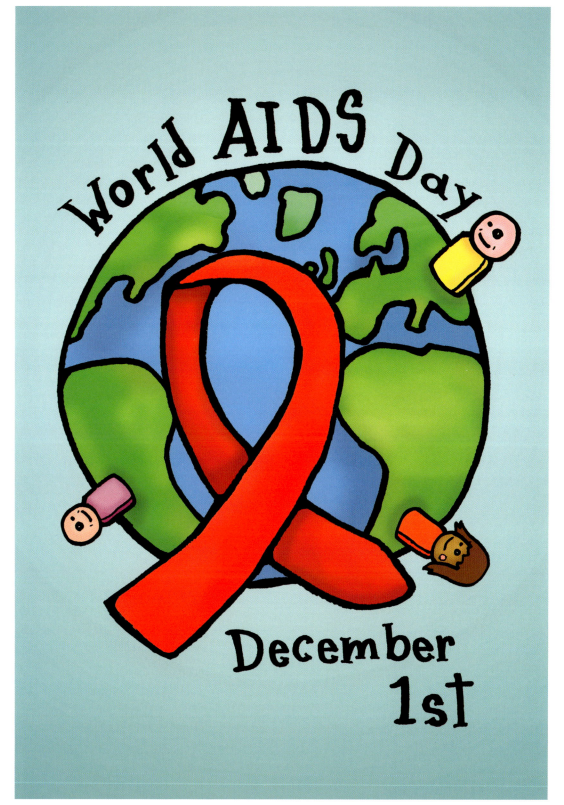

Lucy Rose

lucyplayer@hotmail.com
www.flickr.com/photos/lucyrose

TING
EDGE

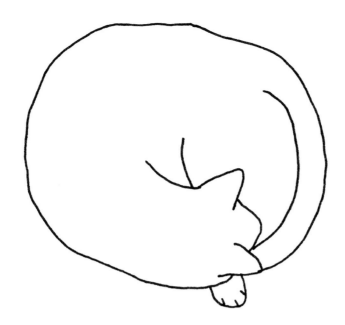

my cat
likes to
sleep like
this.

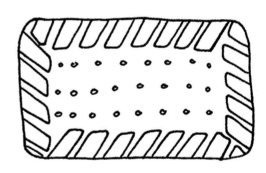

full of beans

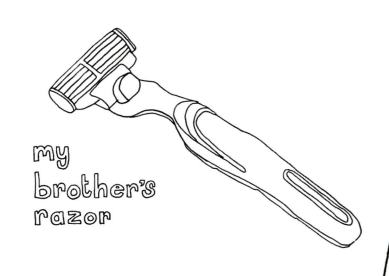

my
brother's
razor

THE ORIGINAL TOUR
London Sightseeing
TOUR
ADULT£019:00
EMBANKMENT PIER
01900   6 4032 4490 1441
16-Sep-07
13:47

* * * * * * * * * *
TODAY'S SERVICE
* * * * Some delays are expected
* * * * * * * * * * *

Tel: +44 (0)20 8877 1722
KEEP YOUR TICKETS SAFE

NOT TRANSFERABLE

BAR
CEL
ONA
10-14 Aug 2008

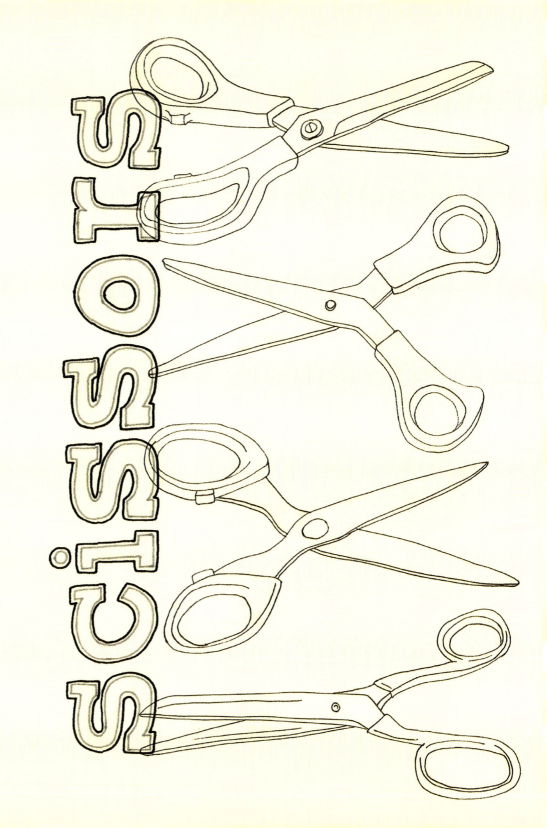

Tony Easley

tony@nascentideas.com
www.vegetablefriedrice.com

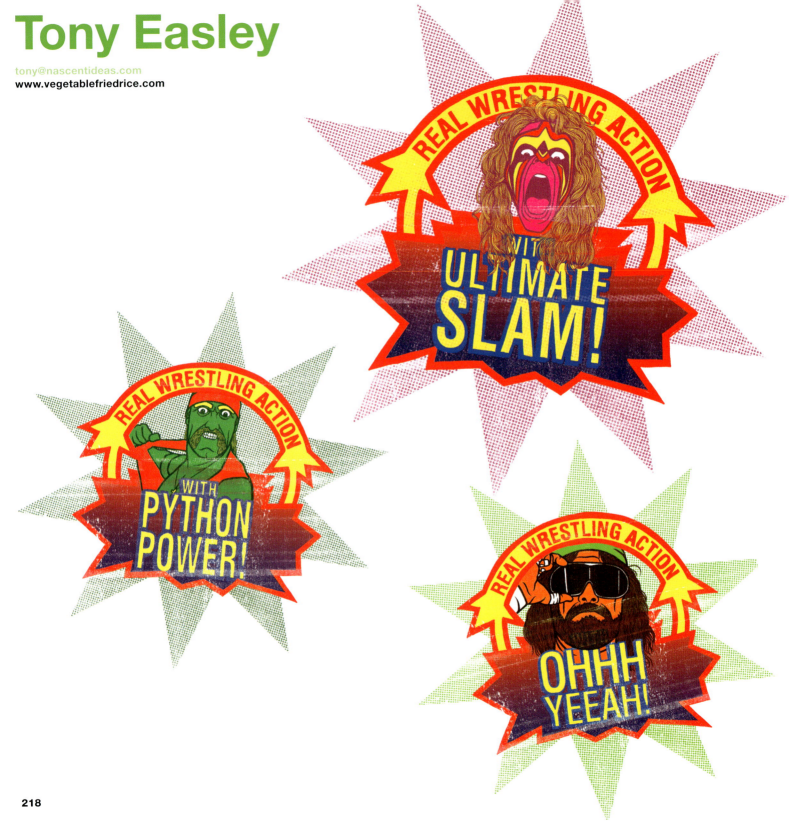

Luke Lucas

luke@lifelounge.com
www.behance.net/Luke_Lucas

CHRIS JORDAN   LORI NIX   SLINKACHU   RANDALL SELLERS   PETER CALLESEN   TINY MASTERS OF TODAY
MAXIMO PARK   BONDE DO ROLÉ   PLEIX   WEEMAN   FRIENDS WITH YOU   MINIATURE HORSES   &   ALL THINGS TINY

the tiny edition

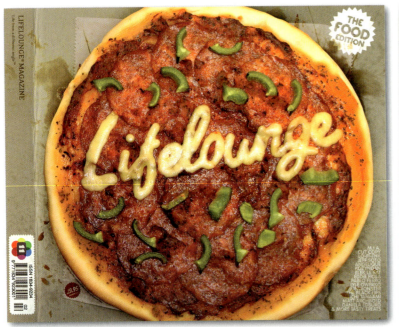

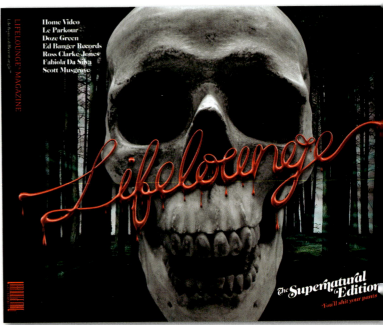

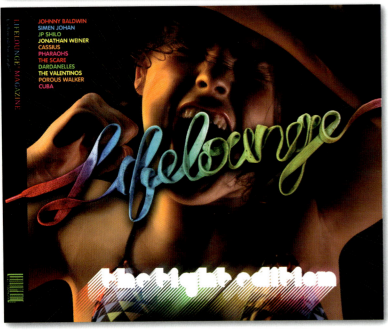

Maxwell Lord

maxxtro@gmail.com
www.86era.org

HEAD x FITTED

Jeffrey Bowman

maxxtro@gmail.com
www.mrbowlegs.co.uk

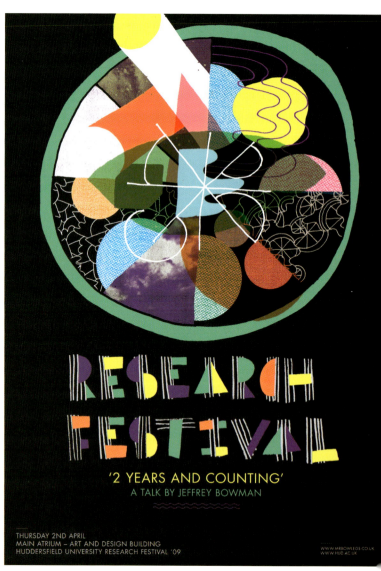

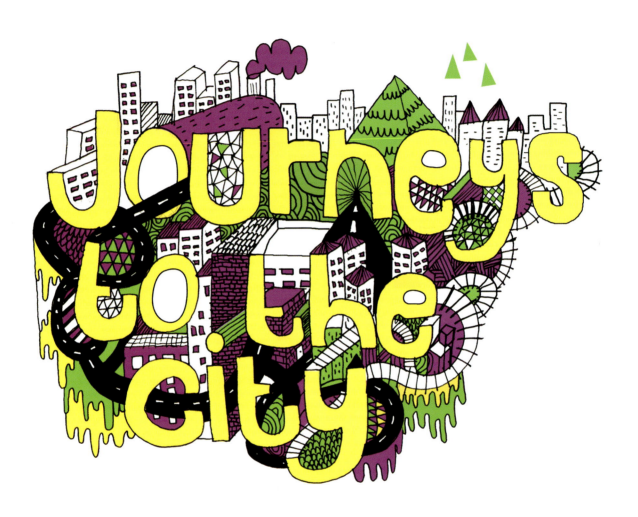

DJ SET'S
THE CINEMA ROOM.

3RD OCTOBER
31ST OCTOBER
28TH NOVEMBER

WWW.MYSPACE.COM/MOONCATSUK
THEMOONCATS@HOTMAIL.CO.UK
DESIGNED BY WWW.MRBOWLEGS.CO.UK
ROCK.ROLL

Andy J.Miller

maxxtro@gmail.com
www.komadesign.co.uk

Chris Haughton

chris@vegetablefriedrice.com
www.vegetablefriedrice.com

Happy Christmas

from (all of us at)

CLEARA.

hello
its me again

and a happy
new year

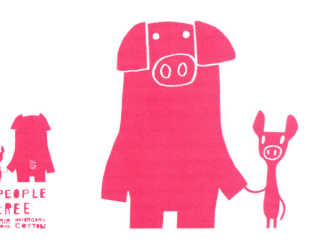

PEOPLE
tREE
FAIR ORGANIC
TRAD COTTON

A BIT LOST.

CHRIS HAUGHTON

Borim ab

Cranberry juice is nice, but it's not an antibiotic.

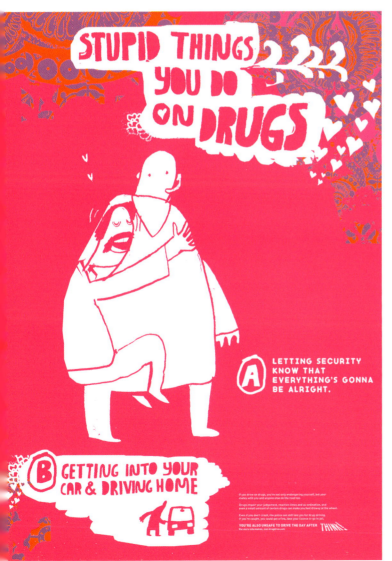

Michael Doret

mhubauer@margarethe.de
www.michaeldoret.com

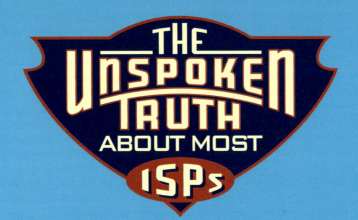

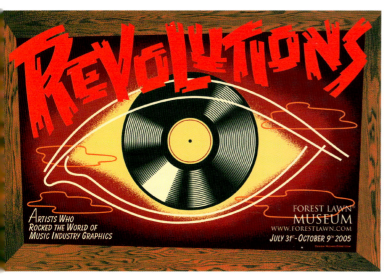

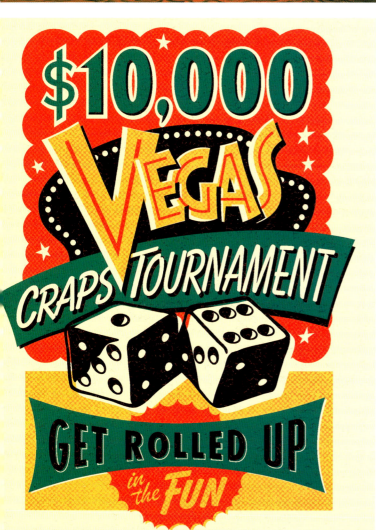

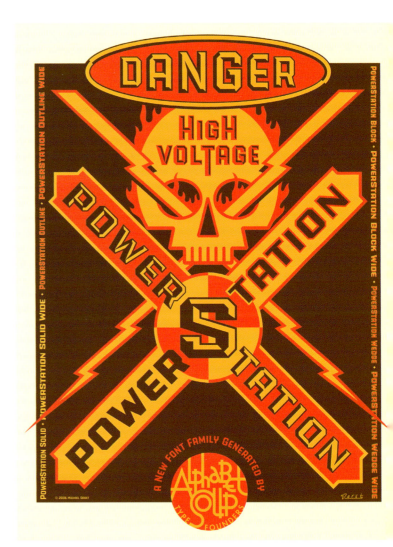

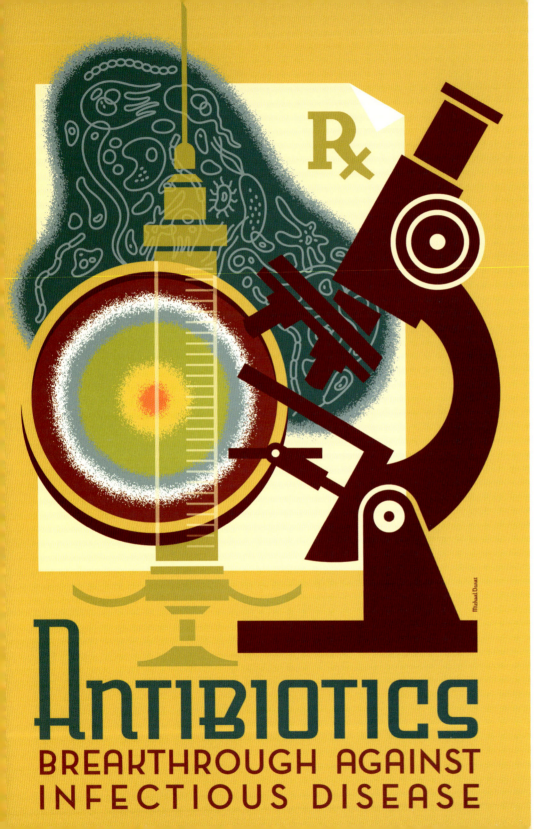

ANTIBIOTICS
BREAKTHROUGH AGAINST INFECTIOUS DISEASE

Frederic Perers

info@fredericperers.cat
www.fredericperers.cat

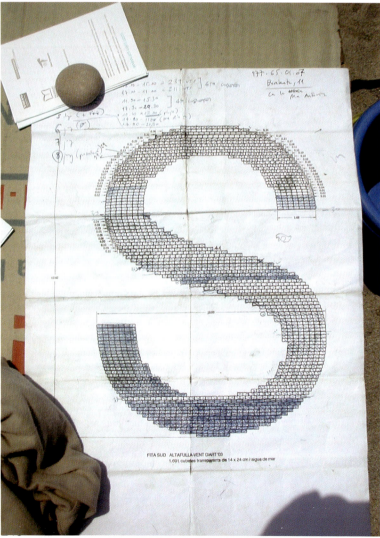

FITA SUD ALTAFULLA-VENT D'ART '03
1.091. cubetes transparents de 14 x 24 cm i aigua de mar

Sergio Jimenez

sergiojimenez@subcoolture.com
www.subcoolture.com

GUAY
COOL
TRENDY
CHACHI

ABCDEFGHIJKLMNÑOPQRSTUVWXYZ

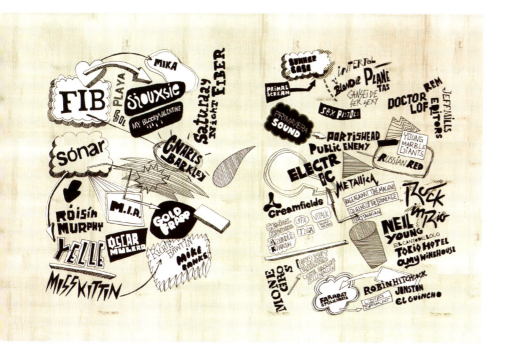

FACEBOOK JUNKIE

JK. Keller

stellar@jk-keller.com
www.c71123.com

get it out
fill it up

fight

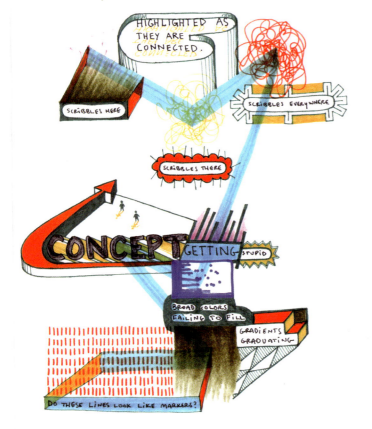

HIGHLIGHTED AS THEY ARE CONNECTED.

SCRIBBLES HERE

SCRIBBLES EVERYWHERE

SCRIBBLES THERE

CONCEPT GETTING STUPID

BROAD COLORS FAILING TO FILL

GRADIENTS GRADUATING

DO THESE LINES LOOK LIKE MARKERS?

immediacy!!

breadth

diligence

I

we

busy work acceptance

yes

ALWAYS TRYING TO PUT OUT my FIRE

fight

if I stand for what's right, you'll almost never put me out.

depth

experimentation

here

hope

new

first

ritual

honesty

maybe we could TALK about it

another GRAY DAY 2

the calculated efforts of the endeavor are at their... what?!? well, i am trying to say that my brain isn't allowing me to do what i want to do. it's calculating too much. it's trying too hard. i guess i want to say some-thing about this. should i create taglines?

i am too self-conscious of the process. Everything must be perfect. i am paralyzing myself. Perhaps it's just too ambitious. i will not allow myself to do some-thing as un-thought-of as this: well, that seems so free! But maybe i can take solace in the fact that i will stick it out + perhaps i will start to relinquish control to the in time... frustration will set maybe you could take solace in the fact that you don't know how to spell.

WIDOWS level
DO
do it all

261

Jackline

whatiswhatnot@yahoo.ca
www.flickr.com/photos/jaclynejaclyne

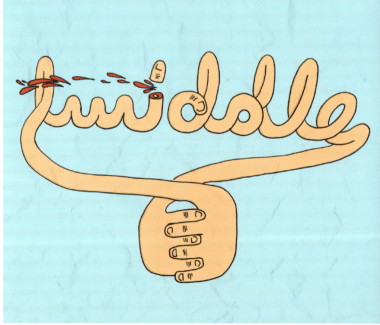

DON'T EXPECT EVERYTHING TO BE HANDED TO YOU ON A SILVER PLATTER. SOMETIMES IT'S MADE OF GOLD

Niels Shoe

info@fredericperers.cat
www.nielsshoemeulman.com

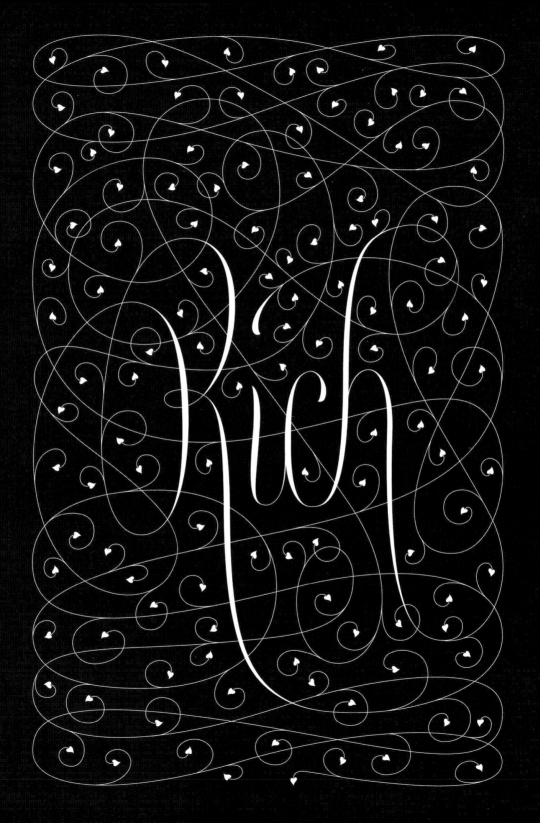

A PICTURE IS WORTH A THOUSAND WORDS

Alex Camacho

mail@alexcamacho.es
www.alexcamacho.es

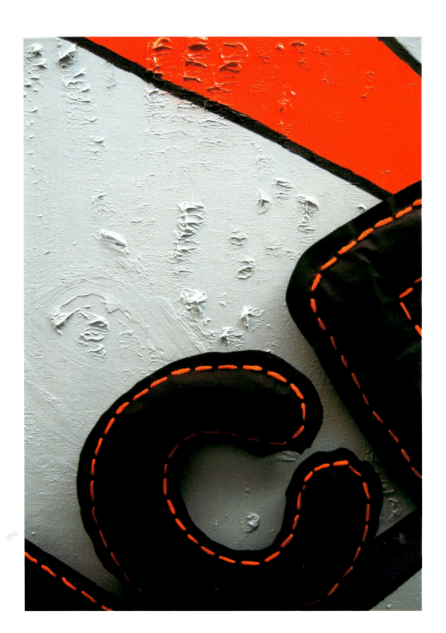

ERRATIC TYPOGRAPHY

NEW OBJECTIVITY

THE ULTIMATE GOAL OF ALL

VISUAL ARTS IS

CONSTRUCTION

THE CREATION AND LOVE OF

BEAUTY ARE ESSENTIAL TO

TO THE HAPPINESS

ART ITSELF CAN NOT BE

TAUGHT BUT CRAFTSMAN

SHIP CAN

WALTER GROPIUS

GOD IS IN THE DETAILS

MIES VAN DER ROHE

THE STYLES ARE A LIE

LE CORBUSIER

BAUHAUS SCHOOL

WEIMAR · DESSAU · BERLIN

STAGES IN GERMANY

BETWEEN 1919 - 1933

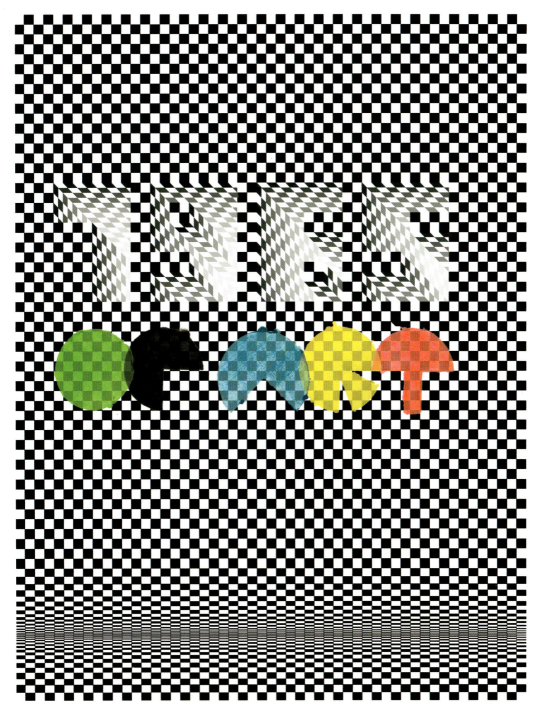

1965
The Responsive Eye

my
new favorite
cupcake

vanilla spelt w/
creamy vanilla frosting
(agave sweetened)

DAIRY, EGG & SOY FREE

at babycakes.
LOWER EAST SIDE, NYC

I was far from home, and so lonely

smell 'em!

TRICK or TREAT

(stinky!)

Smell my FEET

Give me something good to EAT

Kit Kat
CRISP WAFERS IN CHOCOLATE
NET WT 1.5 OZ (42g)

like this

or this

Peter Paul Almond Joy

adi

Simon Palmieri

simon@anekdot.be
www.anekdot.be

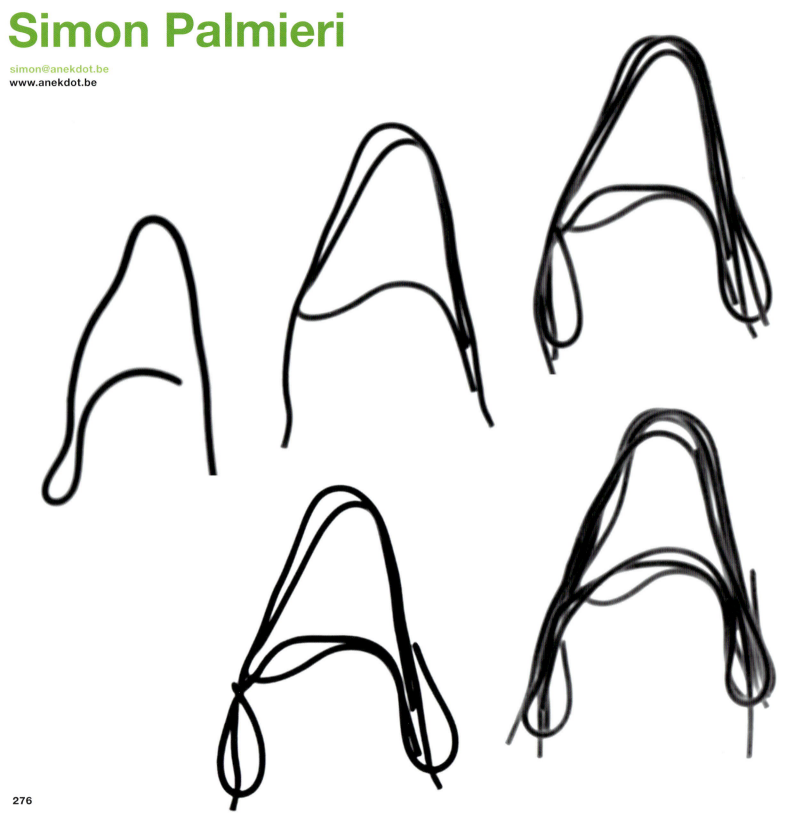

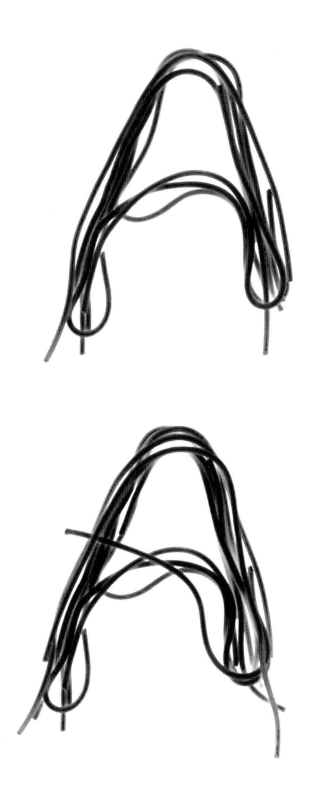
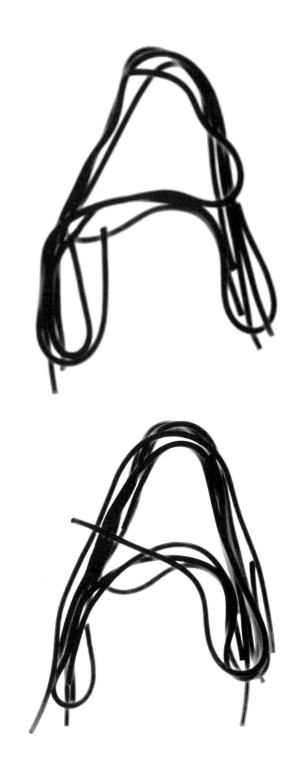

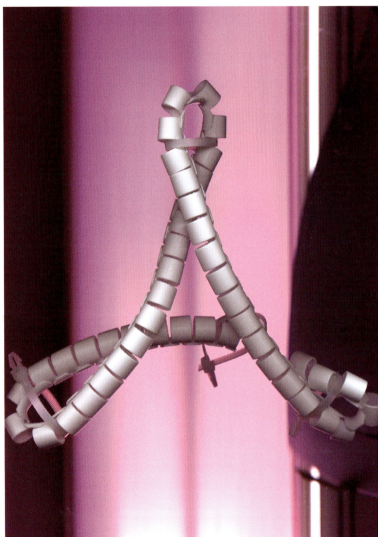

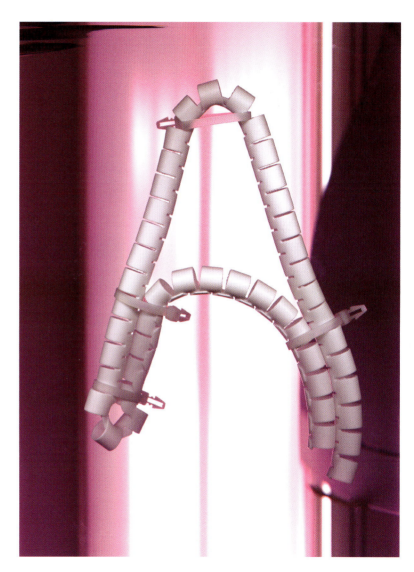

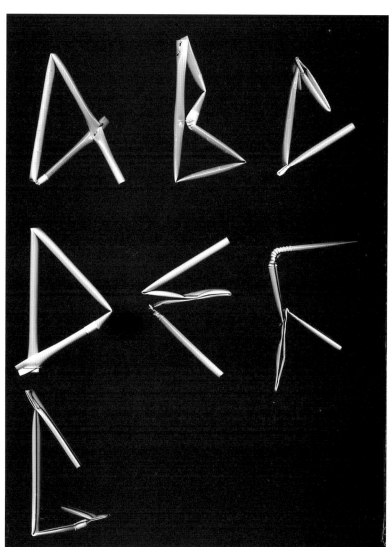

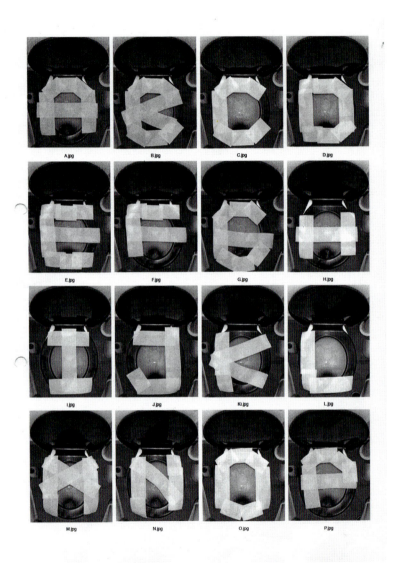

Carmen Burgess

leonesenchina@gmail.com
www.flickr.com/photos/burguess

CARMEN BURGUESS
(VON MUERAN HUMANOS)
PUPPEN & KOLLAGEN
VON 20/12/08 BIS 30/12/08

GALERIE WALLYWOODS

VERNISSAGE 20-12-08 MIT **LIVE KONZERT** VON:

MUERAN HUMANOS + JEMEK JEMOWIT + MAR SHY SUN

BERLINER ALLEE 125 - WEISSENSEE - BERLIN

TRAMS VON ALEX M4 . M13 , M12 BIS BERLINER ALLEE /
INDIRA GANDHI STR .

WWW . CARMENBURGUESS . COM

MISS VERGNUEGEN PRESENTS:
LIVE!

MUERAN HUMANOS

WEDNESDAY
FEBRUARY
18TH

DJs:
MISS
VERGNUEGEN
& MR. B
THE SPECTACULAR
SOUND OF QUEEZY
LISTENING MUSIC
AGAINST
THE
WINTERDEPRESSION
myspace.com/gpunkteffekt

AT ESCHSCHLORAQUE
ROSENTHALER STR. 39
MITTE - BERLIN

myspace.com/mueranhumanos
www.eschschloraque.de

FEBRUARY
6TH
FRIDAY

21 PM
LIVE:
MUERAN HUMANOS
+
So Low Suicide

DJ set
Velvet Condom

LÜBBENER STR. 19
Kreuzberg Berlin

myspace.com/mueranhumanos
myspace.com/solowsuicide

MADAME CLAUDE
myspace.com/madame_claude

MUERAN HUMANOS

"COSMÉTICOS PARA CRISTO"
TOUR 2009
ARGENTINA - URUGUAY

22, ABRIL EN MARQUEE CAP FED
C/ MUTERCITAS TERROR Y BEACH BREAKERS

1º MAYO EN TÍO BIZARRO BURZACO
C/ KWB DER KLANG Y DJ SET DE TRAVESTI

8 DE MAYO EN TÍO BIZARRO, BURZACO
EL MATÓ A UN POLICÍA MOTORIZADO Y VIVA ELÁSTICO

14 DE MAYO EN UNA CASA, CAP FED
C/ VIVA LA MUERTE

16, DE MAYO EN EL LIVING, MONTEVIDEO
C/ FIESTA ANIMAL

Natalia Zaratiegui

nataliazaratiegui@gmail.com
www.nzaratiegui.blogspot.com

andtheclockworktrumpets

Le Vian Sonore

Manuel Romero

citizengrey@gmail.com
www.behance.net/citizengrey

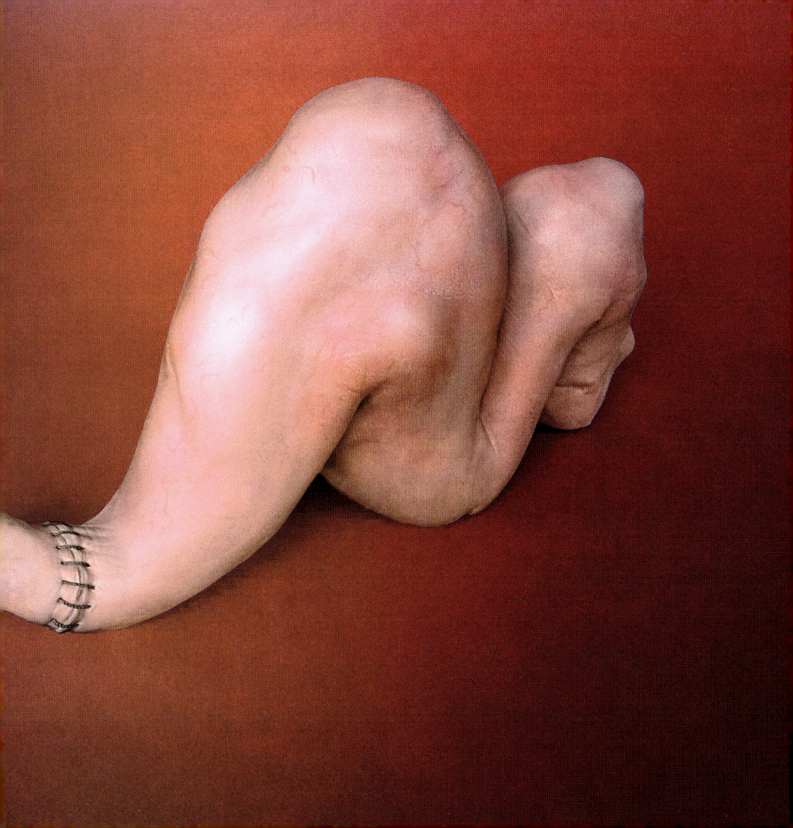

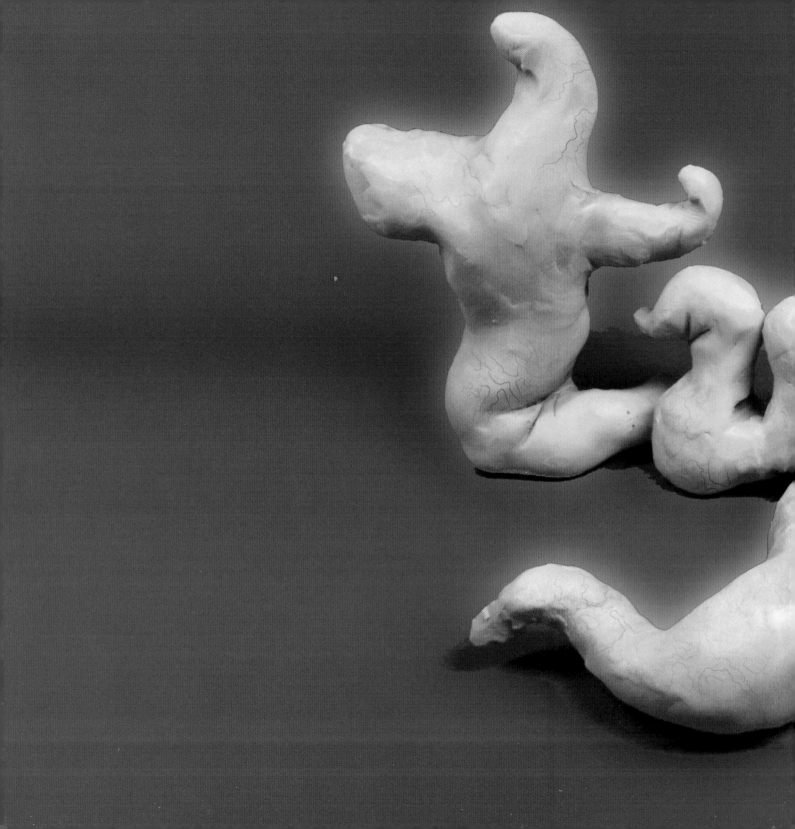

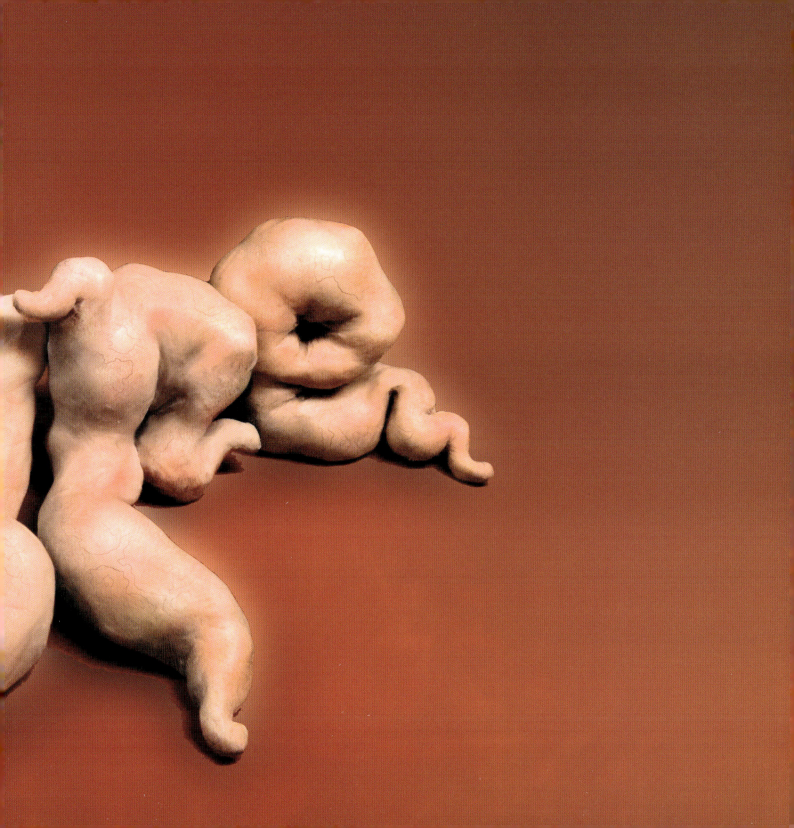